ESSENTIAL KEYS

—◆— FOR —◆—

Marital Success

...short and sweet inspirations

Written by

Osaro Edosa Ogbewe

with

Kathy Bruins

THE WELL
PUBLISHERS

ISBN: 978-1-954658-10-3

Published By:

Name: The Well Publishers

Address: PMB #533, 520 Butternut Dr., Ste. 8, Holland, MI 49424

Email: TheWellPublishers@gmail.com

Cover design by: Oliviaprodesigns

Table of Contents

Dedication

This book is dedicated to Tana Tillis, and to all couples out there.

Appreciation

Appreciation from Osaro:

God has brought this project to fruition after it was conceived over 20 years ago. His timing is **perfect**, and I am so thankful to the Lord.

I thank Dr. Gary Chapman, author of The Five Love Languages for believing in this project and the message therein, and for endorsing and recommending it to anyone seeking happy marriage and relation- ship. Gary, your endorsement means so much to me and to the success of this book. Thank you so much.

Thank **you**, Joanne Hillman, for writing a beautiful and wonderful Fore- word for this book. It took me so much time and effort to get to you and I am happy my effort was rewarded by your positive response to writing this for the book. Your words mean so much to the success of this project and I appreciate you very much.

My heartfelt appreciation and gratitude **go** to Kathy Bruins of Kathy Bruins LLC, Michigan, USA; (www.writingbybruins.com) for touching my life the way she did. "Kathy, thank you so much for doing a great job editing the manuscript and making valuable contributions, thereby turning my little thoughts into a great message. Kathy, you are indeed a motivator and a writer par excellence.

I also appreciate you very much for offering to co-author this book with me and for making this book a high standard for international readers.

Lastly, I thank the people in Nigeria and the United States of America who contributed in one way or another to the success of this book; not leaving out oliviaprodesign from https://www.fiverr.com/ for the beautiful book cover design. May God bless you all for making my dream of many years come to pass.

Appreciation from Kathy

I praise God for the adventure He brings **every day** to us to live out what we believe. His grace is truly sufficient in all things. I thank Him for this opportunity to do Kingdom work.

This truly has been a wonderful journey working on this book with Osaro. I thank him for giving me the opportunity to be a part of it. I appreciate his steadfast faith that shows great trust in God and great love for his fellow man. His marriage is a model of the great love God has for us. I pray blessings over their household for much continued success.

I thank my husband, John, who is always supportive of my work. He has loved me at my best and worst. I am thankful that he was created just for me.

Foreword

It is an honor to be invited to write a foreword for Mr. Osaro Ogbewe's new book, *Essential Keys for Marital Success*. In these pages, he gives fifty-one easy, yet very practical, suggestions for enhancing one's relationship with their spouse. The book is meant to be read slowly, thoughtfully, and prayerfully. I can imagine the renewal of mutual love and joy if these are applied—perhaps one a day or even one each week.

Mr. Ogbewe's sensitivity to the needs of women is particularly amazing. We need to hear loving words often, and these bless us even more when they are coupled with small acts of tenderness and understanding. In turn, men's natural need for respect is filled to overflowing when their wives show them the honor herein described.

Divorce leaves a lasting wound on our hearts, not only to both spouses, but also to their children, their families, and the church of Jesus. I pray that this little guidebook will be used by pastors and counselors to help more Christians overcome their marital unhappiness and find the blessedness our Heavenly Father intends.

Joanne Hillman, author A Perfect Marriage (of two imperfect people); Song of Salome (Jesus as seen by His family and friends); and Patrick and the Prince (a Christian allegory for children).

http://www.joannehillman.com/

Introduction

Marriage is a sexual contract, a covenant between two people and Almighty God, made in front of invited witnesses – a contract to a lifetime of sexual exclusivity.

- Tim LaHaye

What needs to happen for a marriage to be happy and successful? I am sure many answers may come to your mind for we each have different life experiences. Yet, there are common practices in building relationships to make them stronger that work. This book is going to discuss the keys to having a successful marriage and being a happy spouse. *Essential Keys for Marital Success* will equip anyone who is committed to working on their marriage and making it better.

Statistics show that 40 to 50 percent of marriages end in divorce. This is common knowledge and almost an expectation. That would be like looking down your street and imagining every other neighbor's household will have a divorce! Divorce is a devastating occurrence, not only to the couple, but also to children and other family members. Although I am presently happily married, I know firsthand that divorce is a devastating experience as I have experienced a divorce in the past. It truly made me sad to go through it, and I do not want anyone else to suffer like that, which is why I am so passionate about this topic. Divorce is not an easy way out as many seem to think. Sometimes it can be more work and stress than if the couple decided to try and work things out. The result could be a lot better.

I invite you to choose the better way. The divorce rate is not God's plan for marriage. Many couples who do decide to stay together are miserable in the marriage for they have not taken steps to fix whatever is happening between the two. Marriage is not to be endured but enjoyed! The Lord doesn't want you to be suffering in a marriage either. He has a better way. This book will reflect the fruit of the Spirit in building your marriage with your mate, and not cutting it down. If you choose to do nothing to better your relationship, then you have already given up on making it successful. I pray that you will hear the call of God on your heart to save your marriage. I want to be clear that this is not suggesting that anyone stay in an abusive situation. Sometimes separation needs to happen, but in most cases, the divisions couples experience can be worked out. What are you willing to give to have marital success?

The keys included will cover topics such as communication, active listening, helping your mate, kissing, sex, the power of words, respect, and much more. Each chapter begins with a carefully chosen quote that will welcome you into the discussion. The book is laid out so that it will be easy for you to pick up at any time and read any short chap- ter. As you read the chapter, try to imagine yourself attempting the key that is suggested. The next step will be to put it into action. Some of the tasks of the chapters may feel uncomfortable to do at first, or very fun, but once you begin and you see the response of your spouse, you will want to continue. The illustrations provided will really help to drive home the message being conveyed. The benefits of using the keys and doing the actions prescribed in this book are many. Your marriage will be better, plus you model for other marriages how to be truly happy together. Children need this positive impression of witnessing your love and care for your mate. You will be leaving a legacy of love.

I believe the divorce rate can be greatly reduced if we make work of strengthening marriage and caring for one another. No marriage is perfect, so please don't feel yours is a failure if it doesn't measure up to others. Your relationship with your spouse is unique, just as everyone is unique. God's plan for you as a couple will look different than the plan he has for another. But remember that his plan for you and for your marriage is good.

"For I know the plans I have for you," declares the Lord, "plans to prosper you and not to harm you, plans to give you hope and a future," (Jeremiah 29:11).

Essential Keys for Marital Success is highly also recommended for singles who are preparing for marriage. They will find this book very interesting and useful. In fact, I urge everyone preparing for marriage to read this book to equip them for the journey of marriage. There is something to learn in this book, no matter who you are or how old you are.

I make bold to say these keys have greatly helped my marriage! It can help yours too.

I will be ending each chapter with a heartfelt blessing:

May God bless your home, and keep your marriage ... in Jesus' name, Amen.

Chapter 1: Start with a Kiss

Kissing is a means of getting two people so close together that they can't see anything wrong with each other.

- Rene Yasenek

Like the song says, "You must remember this … A kiss is just a kiss, a sigh is just a sigh. The fundamental things apply … As time goes by." This song became a romantic classic from the movie Casablanca. In those days, you weren't sure if the actors were going to kiss. The scene would move towards that, but sometimes they didn't reach the goal, or they would switch the screen to show a shadow of the actors kissing. Perhaps this was to build on the excitement of the moment. The old classics are definitely different than today's movies. How times have changed. At the start of a relationship, there is an inward excitement, a building anticipation towards the other person, and when you kiss them the first time, your heart pounds and your toes curl. You can't wait until the next time you kiss them. You may feel that way for a while, but then one day, it seems to become routine. The electricity you felt before disappeared. What happened to it? The lips you once were nervous about kissing are now "no big deal." They are taken for granted.

Busyness in your life as a married couple may be causing you to focus on other areas of life rather than on your spouse. There are jobs and careers, children to care for, family and friends, housework, education, and more. Many temptations beckon you in this world, and you are constantly distracted. It becomes difficult just to be creative like you once were with your love. It's not too late to get yourself back into the old days of the romantic kiss with your spouse. You can relive the excitement of kissing in several ways.

1. Reminisce about the first time you kissed your spouse. Think about your feelings and the excitement of the moment. Remember how you prepared yourself to be ready? Good breath, clean teeth, and moist lips were on the checklist. You took the time and effort to be as perfect as you could so you would not offend your date. You may have even practiced your kissing techniques in front of the mirror. Bottom line is that it was important to you.

2. Just do it! Give your spouse a kiss first thing in the morning, and throughout the day as the opportunities arise. Nothing says, "Good morning, darling. I love you," like a kiss at the beginning of the day. The message is refreshed throughout the day as more kisses are added. A kiss says, "I love you and you are important to me."

3. Take your time with the kiss. It is not a race (unless you want to see who can kiss the longest). Partner it with snuggling or a hug or other respectful touching. Hold their face gently and look in their eyes intently. That will leave a memory in your love's heart and mind that they will never forget.

4. Try different methods of kissing such as French kissing. Add some spark to the kisses. To French kiss, gently part your spouse's lips with the tip of your tongue. Do not force your whole tongue in their mouth at once. Be passionate, but not forceful. The key is respect.

5. Find out the favorite places your spouse likes to be kissed. Some say the wrist, arms and neck can be sensitive favorites. Enjoy discovering your spouse's titillating areas that send tingles through their spine.

6. Pretend you are in a romantic movie, and you have to be convincing and pull off the part of the ardent lover in the kissing scene. Have fun with it. If you need help, review movie classics with Richard Gere, Brad Pitt, Errol Flynn, Valentino and other male leads, or female leads such as Angelina Jolie, Sharon Stone, Marilyn Monroe, Lauren Bacall or other.

7. Read aloud to your spouse the Scripture from Song of Solomon that talks about kisses. Things may heat up for both of you by reading these passionate romantic writings. *"Let him kiss me with the kisses of his mouth: for thy love is better than wine"* (Song of Solomon 1:2).

In the Bible, there are many references to kisses. The kiss was an important symbol of love and friendship. Charles Spurgeon said in a devotional writing, "By kisses we supposed to be intended those varied manifestations of affection by which the believer is made to enjoy the love of Jesus."[1] This quote shows how awful it was for Jesus when Judas betrayed him with a kiss. A symbol of total love and devotion was used as a tool of evil.

Do you take the symbolism of a kiss seriously? It represents your heart, displaying every day your love to your spouse in the act of a kiss. Don't make it a simple brush across the lips or a quick peck but put your heart into it. Where do you think your spouse would rate you now in regard to kissing on a scale of one to ten? Where would you like to be on the scale and what are you willing to do to make that happen? Marriage is sacrifice, but in a good way. Giving to the person you love the best of yourself is honoring to God.

Kissing can be exceptionally magical. Starting each day with a kiss could be likened to taking daily marriage pills for marriage success. Many couples find this difficult to do, but it is strongly advised, and statistics have shown that couples who engage in the act of kissing, particularly before they go to bed along with welcoming the other person home, are happier together and less likely to contemplate divorce than couples who do not. A kiss works like medicine. Try it and see your marriage receiving new life.

May God bless your home, and keep your marriage ... in Jesus' name, Amen.

---

[1] Spurgeon, C. H. *Morning and evening: Daily readings* (Peabody, MA: Hendrickson Publishers Complete and unabridged; New modern edition, 2006).

Chapter 2: Remember the Message of the Ring

Your gift to me is uninsurable. No appraiser can put a value on it... It's like fruit of the month or a lifetime subscription – a perpetual-motion happiness machine. It starts off fresh and brand new every day, shining up my whole world...

- Ronald Reagan – in a letter to his wife Nancy

Allysa throws the pillows off the couch along with the cushions. She digs inside the couch and finds nothing. Where is her ring? She remembers taking it off last night while watching a movie and putting it in her shirt pocket, but it isn't there. It fell out somewhere.

She hears her husband, Raul, pull into the driveway. Quickly, putting the cushions back on the couch and arranging the pillows, she sits down not wanting anything to be amiss. It is uncertain how Raul will react to the news. He probably will be upset like her.

The door opens and Raul enters. He put down his briefcase, took off his coat and hangs it up. He walks over to the couch and sits by Allysa.

Giving her a kiss, he then asks, "How was your day today?" Allysa burst into tears.

"Honey, what is it? Did someone die?" He tries to console her.

She shakes her head. "No, but I did something terrible. I lost my wedding ring." After giving the news, another torrent of tears come.

Raul laughs and hugs Allysa. "I am so relieved it is just that … I thought you had some really bad news."

Allysa stops crying. She sits up and says, "What?"

"It's just a ring. I will buy you another one."

She looks at him as if she didn't know him. "It's just a ring? It's just a ring?" She stands up and goes upstairs to their bedroom and slams the door.

******

God flooded the earth destroying all of creation. He made a promise to Noah and to us that never again would this happen. The promise was sealed with a rainbow.

> And God said, "This is the guarantee of the covenant I am making with you and every living creature with you, a covenant for all subsequent generations: I will place my rainbow in the clouds, and it will become a guarantee of the covenant between me and the earth. Whenever I bring clouds over the earth and the rainbow appears in the clouds, then I will remember my covenant with you and with all living creatures of all kinds. Never again will the waters become a flood and destroy all living things. When the rainbow is in the clouds, I will notice it and remember the perpetual covenant between God and all living creatures of all kinds that are on the earth."[2]

Promises are important because that is what you base your trust on. If someone makes you a promise, and then breaks it, your trust in them will fall to a lower level. However, if someone has made a pattern of fulfilling their

---

[2] *The NET Bible First Edition; Bible. English. NET Bible* (Biblical Studies Press, 2006), Genesis 9:12–16.

promises, your trust in them is elevated. God has always fulfilled his promises and that's why you can trust the Lord completely.

The wedding ring continues to be a symbol of promise much like the rainbow. In the ring, there is no beginning or end … it just continues. This symbol gives confidence to you and your spouse that the vows professed on their wedding day are still true today. The ring is a reminder. You need that reminder. Wedding rings are not essential to be married. It is a tradition to use them. It is a tradition that you feel secure in. The rings display the message that you are committed to a life-long relationship with your spouse. That's why it is so devastating to go through a divorce and remove the ring from your hand showing the commitment was not true. It is heartbreaking not only to you, but to God.

Take a moment and look closely at your wedding ring. Do you remember having it slipped onto your finger and special words of love and commitment said at the same time? How do you feel wearing your wedding ring every day? Are you proud of the commitment you've made, or do you wish it would vanish and leave your marital status a mystery? The way you answer this question reflects on the type of commitment you made that day. If you are truly committed to your spouse, wear your ring proudly. Show your spouse that the ring is important to you. This will give your marriage partner confidence of your commitment to them.

An article in "Wedding Vendors" regarding wedding rings and their symbolism states that, "Wedding rings capture the full range of the ceremonial, symbolic, and communal aspects of marriage, and preserve these many levels of significance as a durable and constant reminder. Ancient yet contemporary, steeped in lore and mystery yet almost universally exchanged, wedding rings combine the art of the

jeweler, the reverence of the betrothed, and the beauty of love and partnership in a single, resonant symbol."[3] It truly holds much significance in a marriage

---

[3] Peter Breslin, *Symbolism of Wedding Rings,*
http://www.weddingven-
dors.com/planning/articles/symbolism-wedding-rings/, July 5,
2005.

and has for centuries. Making wedding rings out of gold or silver is symbolic of using a precious metal that was durable, just like the marriage would be.

The key is to show that your promise to your spouse is important today as it was the day you made the vow. Your wedding ring is a symbol of that, so show its importance in your life.

May God bless your home, and keep your marriage ... in Jesus' name, Amen.

Chapter 3: Schedule Regular Date Nights

Coming together is a beginning; keeping together is pro- gress; working together is success.

- Henry Ford

"Mommy, where are you and daddy going?"

Nan is putting on a necklace when the question is asked. She smiles at the confused look on her daughter's round face. "Daddy and I are going on a date."

"But you're married already."

"Yes, we are, but that doesn't mean we need to stop dating, does it?"

"I guess not, but aren't you too old to date?"

"No, we are not honey"!

******

What did you do on a date before you became married? Was the actual date more important or just being with the person you were dating? Probably the latter. Now as you enjoy your married years, you can both still date each other and focus on whatever activity you choose while enjoying each other's company, too.

You realize, of course, that just because you married someone doesn't mean that you know all about them. You have a lifetime of learning about your spouse. At times, you will be surprised on how they react or respond to something. Like you, they are continually growing and changing as you both mature. This keeps life exciting. Life experiences mold you into the person God wants you to become. You are not the same person you were years ago. Someone once said, "The moment you stop growing, you start dying." This is also true of relationships. Date night is important. You learned about each other in your early dating years. Now you have opportunities to learn more about your mate. Be aware of the changes they are going through. You grow closer as you learn more about your mate.

Jesus knew it was important to spend time with the disciples, so they basically came to live with him wherever he went. He walked with them morning, noon, and night. "After this, Jesus and his disciples came into Judean territory, and there he spent time with them and was baptizing" (John 3:22). They witnessed Jesus do all sorts of ministry. The disciples learned who Jesus was … as much as they could anyways. They only had three years of doing ministry with him.

You have a lifetime to get to know your spouse. Look for something new about them every day. On your dates, ask questions that will help you know more about them such as, "What are the best three things that happened to you today?" You want to ask questions that can't be answered by a yes or no, so that you can get more information. Discover how they feel about issues, what makes them sad, or how they feel appreciated. There are an infinite number of things you can find out about them that will enrich your marriage and truly help you to feel that you have married your best friend.

What to do on a date

Keep in mind that the goal is not only to have an enjoyable time, but to get to know one another better. Going to a movie prohibits any talking, but perhaps you could go for coffee and ice cream afterward and discuss the film. Be adventurous as you discover new things together. Here are some possibilities for you and your spouse to do together:

- Going for a nice dinner and talking
- Hiking or climbing a mountain

- Canoeing or snorkeling
- Wine tasting
- Go to a carnival or fair that may be in town
- Antiquing
- Riding bikes
- Playing tennis
- Laying on the beach
- Sailing
- Concert or symphony
- Take a class together
- Learn to dance together, and then do it regularly
- Take the dog for a nice long walk. Don't have a dog? You might need one.
- Exercise together
- Make a romantic meal together. Have soft lights and music to set the mood.

This is a short list of the possibilities. Perhaps together with your spouse, you could think of more to do. Make it fun. It doesn't need to be perfect, in fact, if it doesn't turn out well at all, that's okay. The main goal is doing something together.

Date night should be on the calendar each week. This gives you both something to look forward to during the week. Dating may feel weird once you get started, but as time goes on you will both feel very comfortable with each other. It's a special time where you both say, "You're important and I want to spend time with you." The results will be fabulous. Try it!

May God bless your home, and keep your marriage ... in Jesus' name, Amen.

Chapter 4: You Have Differences ... Accept Them

Once we figured out that we could not change each other, we became free to celebrate ourselves as we are.

- H. Dean Rutherford (in a letter to his wife on their 59th wedding anniversary)

Oil and vinegar don't mix; however, it makes for a wonderful tasting salad. It is also true for the differences you have with others, especially your spouse. You were not created to be a robot to think and do the same thing everyone else is doing. God in his creative wisdom made you unique. You can celebrate that.

When you married your spouse, you may have felt that you had so much in common that they must be the right person. They are the right person, but it may not be only what you have in common, but what you don't. Opposites attract and there is probably something in your spouse's makeup that is attractive to you. Are there differences you don't like? That's okay. Those differences are being used to shape your relationship. In clothing, you may be a brown, navy and black conservative, and your spouse may enjoy wearing bright colors. Together you balance each other out. Your spouse livens up your outfit, while you tone their outfit down. It may entice you to try clothes that add a bit of color to your outfit, or you may influence your spouse to try a more conservative look.

Let's say that your family background was dysfunctional and your spouse's wasn't. Because of the life experiences that were different, you may feel disconnected with sharing in family events, while your spouse is fully engaged. I believe God ordained these differences so that one could help the other heal from their past wounds.

Read the book of Ruth in the Bible. Boaz and Ruth came from different lands and were married. Ruth was a Moabite and Boaz came from the line of Judah. I can guarantee there were differences between the way they lived, but it made them stronger as a couple. In fact, the kind hearts that were displayed by both Ruth (towards her mother-in- law Naomi) and Boaz (for supplying safety and provision for Ruth) were honoring to God. The Lord blessed them and made them part of the lineage of Jesus.

"Opposites stretch us beyond ourselves, forcing us to broaden our horizons. They add depth and provide opportunities for growth. It's from them that we learn our most difficult lessons. They expose us to thoughts, feelings, and experiences that are foreign to us. They balance our lopsidedness and make us more complete." (Dr. Steve Stevens)[4] Differences help you think outside of the box. You may have always thought one way on an issue, but your spouse may have a totally different outlook on it. Their opinion forces you to think more on the issue and expand your horizons on how you really feel about it. Debate is good for the mind. It strengthens your thinking power. It's beneficial to have a spouse who is different than you. For example, if you buy an item the moment you see it simply because you want it, you may have be an impulse buyer. If your spouse is more cautious in spending money and will consider all the facts before purchasing, this may help you not overspend or buy something you really don't want or need.

A detail-oriented person is great to have around when you are a big picture person. You want to conquer the mountain, and they can tell you how best to

---

[4] Dr. Steve Stephens, "Accepting Differences – Marriage Message #110" Marriage Missions International, http://marriagemissions.com/accepting-differences-marriage-message-110/, (August 2010).

do it. This would save you from wrong moves and accelerate the procession to the goal.

Differences can also help you discern what is most important. You may never come to an agreement on an issue with your spouse. What does that mean for your relationship? What is more important? Is it the issue or your marriage? Sometimes you must pick the mountains to die on. If it is not that big of an issue, let it go. If it is bigger, then work together to find a way to agree, even if it means to agree to disagree for now. It's important to keep communicating your feelings on a subject. That's what a good marriage is all about … good communication.

There's a couple I know that go to different churches because they don't agree on where they are being called to do in ministry. One feels the smaller church needs them, or the church will die. The other feels called to be more involved in ministry and the smaller church doesn't have that mission in their statement. This does not meet the heart needs of the spouse who wants to become active in ministry. Their differences in opinion will be a blessing for both churches, and as they walk through this time, they are going to discover to intentionally connect and discuss the sermons and other parts of each service. They will continue to grow and mature in their faith.

It's important to communicate your appreciation of the many ways your spouse is different than you. Thank them for how they help you see things differently. You appreciate the different viewpoints and learn from them.

Do not try to make your spouse just like you. That would be going against God's original plan for them, and it does not make for a happy household. God does want unity, but he will journey with both of you to get there.

If you and your spouse's difference are focused inside yourselves, you fight for them. However, spouses that stand in unity use their differences to support one another and battle challenges in life. Showing appreciation for your spouse's differences will make them feel supported and loved. All of us who are married should do this to make our marriage stronger.

May God bless your home, and keep your marriage … in Jesus' name, Amen.

Chapter 5: Politeness Goes a Long Way

And in the end, the love you take is equal to the love you make.

- John Lennon and Paul McCartney

Shannon just returned home from getting groceries and saw her husband in the hammock. She thought, oh good ... there are so many bags, his help would be so appreciated. She got out of the car and her husband said, "Hi Honey, I'm just getting a few rays."

"Okay, I got a ton of groceries."

"That's good. Love to have the frig full."

He didn't make any attempt to get up and help. So she said, "Yes, that would be good. Some of these bags are quite full and heavy."

"You must have found some good deals." He remained in the hammock.

Shannon picked up the lawn hose and pointed the sprayer at her husband and pulled the trigger. He jumped off the hammock as the cold water hit him.

"Oh good, you're up. Now you can help me bring groceries in the house."

******

When you first meet someone, you put your best foot forwards; you want to make a good impression. As you become closer to the person, you normally relax on the formalities and show more of your regular personality. Unfortunately, when you do this, politeness also fades, because you may figure that the niceties aren't necessary anymore. What used to be, "At your convenience, could you please pass the potatoes?" has turned into, "Pass the potatoes." In your mind, it may seem like the same message, because the other one knows you well enough to understand what you mean, and you don't have to be polite anymore. Wrong!

Even though you are married, you are still two individuals that need the same respect as before. Courtesy is needed in all interactions between you both because you both deserve it. Not being polite is demeaning to your spouse. It exhibits that you care less about them than the time you were dating. Doesn't it make sense that the more time you spend together, now that you are man and wife, should be enhanced with politeness? More grace is needed when people spend a lot of time together, or tenseness could develop. You may love the other person completely, but they could still get on your nerves or vice versa. I think of the character, Robert, in the television show *Everybody Loves Raymond*. He always had to touch his chin with food before eating it. That is a quirk that would drive anyone crazy. Even his wife, Amy, who loved him very much was eventually maddened by the behavior and wanted it to be corrected. She always tried to be polite in showing her concern regarding the "chin thing" when she talked to him about it. This helped Robert be able to hear what she was saying rather than only reacting.

I imagine when the disciples were around Jesus so much during his ministry that they may have gotten on his nerves now and then. Jesus knew he needed a break at times with his Father and would go off and be alone. "The next day the crowd that remained on the other side of the lake realized that only one small boat had been there, and that Jesus had not boarded it with his disciples, but that his disciples had gone away alone."[5] Everyone needs a break from

---

[5] *NET Bible® copyright ©1996-2006 by Biblical Studies Press, L.L.C. http://net-bible.com.*

someone especially if one feels their polite ways are waning. It's a sign that refreshment is needed.

Think about when you are in a restaurant, and you receive service from a worker with an attitude. It ruins your whole time out. How you are treated matters. That's why so many businesses are putting surveys on your receipt slips. They want to make sure your experience with them was good and that you will come back. It's the same with marriage. Courtesy will bring your spouse closer to you, because the efforts you make to be polite will be drawing, just like we are drawn closer to businesses that exhibit good customer service.

Your spouse is worth way more than a customer, coworker, or anyone else. You made vows to love them until the day you die. When something or someone is more valuable, you give more of yourself to it. You spend more time and energy. Being polite is a gift that is wrapped up with your love. It's unique in today's communication unless someone is trying to sell you something. In fact, if your spouse isn't used to it, they may think you're up to something by the transformation of your personality. By being polite, you are showing that your relationship is highly valued. Politeness keeps you from being harsh or unfeeling. It helps you think before you speak. Many a fight has occurred because of words said that were not thought out well. Save your relationship and be nice every opportunity you are given.

You could make a game of it. When one of you forgets to say "please" or "thank you," then you must pay the other person a quarter. This would be fun along with helping each of you remember to be polite. Perhaps you could use the winnings for a nice gift for your spouse or take them out for coffee or ice cream.

Keep focused on being polite to your mate. It's not what the world does, and that's why it's important that you do. You want to be the safe place for your spouse where they feel comfortable and protected.

"Man is the only animal that learns by being hypocritical. He pretends to be polite and then, eventually, he *becomes* polite" — Jean Kerr, *Finishing Touches*[6]. It might not feel normal at first to be polite to your spouse, but if you keep at it,

---

[6] Merriam-Webster, I. *The Merriam-Webster dictionary of quotations* (Spring- field, MA: Merriam-Webster 1992),

someday it will become a part of who you are. Wanting to treat your spouse in the best possible manner will become natural, which honors God.

May God bless your home, and keep your marriage ... in Jesus' name, Amen.

Chapter 6: Gentle Ben

There is nothing stronger in the world than gentleness.

- Han Suyin

Back in the '60's, there was a television show called Gentle Ben. This show described the relationship of a grizzly bear with a young boy and his family. The boy was the son of game warden in the Florida Everglades, so they did not live in suburbia, but often traveled through the Everglades on an air boat.

The bear was a grizzly, which was often thought of as being ferocious and very dangerous, but in this series, the bear was very gentle and got into mischief. The family loved the bear. Of course, it was a great source of protection for the boy if any bad guys came around. Most of the time though the bear was gentle and fun to be around. The people in the community were drawn to the bear knowing of its gentleness.

There is also something very attractive in someone who is gentle. It's like having the "Aw!" button pushed when a strong man holds a

little newborn. Gentleness takes away fear. Many times, a spouse may feel they have to be rough and tough to be a "real man" or in some cases, a "real woman." This kind of thinking is wrong. A real man displays his gentle side, because he is comfortable with who he is and isn't bothered by what other people think. They just want to be there for their family. They don't want fear to be a factor of having their family with them.

Speaking with gentleness

One of the ways to be gentle is in how you say things. It's important to be honest with your spouse, but it is also important to be honest gently. This will draw your spouse to you and create a trusting and safe environment for them. The key is to really think about what you are going to say before you say it. "Understand this, my dear brothers and sisters! Let every person be quick to listen, slow to speak, slow to anger," (James 1:19).

Here are a couple examples of speaking in gentleness. If your spouse asks you for your opinion on what they are wearing, and you really don't like the outfit, there's a couple of ways you can handle it. You can either use a brutal or gentle response. A brutal response may be something like, "You look like a clown in that outfit," whereas a gentle response may be more like, "It seems to fit you well, but I really liked what you tried on before."

Another example may be if your spouse tries a new recipe. They ask you how you like it. You may brutally answer them with, "My shoe would taste better," or you could be gentle and say, "Honey, it is so wonderful how you try new recipes, like what you made last night was fantastic. That was the best."

The goal is to always build up your marriage partner and never say demeaning things to them. If you are ever abusive to them verbally or physically, an image is created that rarely goes away from their mind. It is there to stay. There is forgiveness where they can freely trust and love again, but it would be impossible to forget the incident ever happened. It becomes part of their mental file that opens when similar incidents happen. They may feel the same fear, anger, or disgust they felt with the original incident. Be very careful not to create negative experiences for your spouse.

Evaluation

At the end of the day, think about all the interactions you had with your spouse. Think about how you could have been gentler with them. Don't knock yourself down if you weren't gentle but consider it a lesson learned that you could use to improve on your communication with your spouse. Commit to trying a better way next time. Your spouse will notice and appreciate it very much.

You will model for your spouse gentleness that they may use on you and others. Many will be blessed by your efforts of being gentle. It can be a "pay it forward" exercise that continues and grows stronger. Your spouse will be proud of you in making gentleness a new normal in your interactions with them and others. Practicing gentleness will soon become natural for you. It may seem uncomfortable or unfamiliar now, but after experiencing positive reactions from your spouse as you are gentle, will encourage you to keep going.

Jesus knew how to be gentle with others. "Take my yoke on you and learn from me, because I am gentle and humble in heart, and you will find rest for your souls," (Matthew 11:29). He called himself gentle for he wanted others to come to him and live better than ever before. He cared about them. Life can be so difficult, but Jesus says that you can take his yoke meaning joining him on the journey of life, walking side by side, and he will lead the way to go and use his power to make it happen. All the efforts you have been using may be tiring you out. Allowing Jesus to take the lead will help you be refreshed and learn that gentleness is powerful and gainful. It will transform your relationship, and indeed your marriage.

May God bless your home, and keep your marriage ... in Jesus' name, Amen.

Chapter 7: Presents Make the Heart Grow Fonder

Love is always bestowed as a gift -freely, willingly, and without expectation. We don't love to be loved, we love to love.

- Leo Buscagalia

Bonnie was surprised to see the red roses in the vase on her desk. Who could have got them for her? Just then, Daniel, an office co-worker came by and admired the flowers.

"Did you read the card to see who they were from?" he asked.

"I didn't see a card."

Just then, Daniel pulled from his pocket the card.

"There from you? But why?"

"Just read the card, Bonnie."

She opened it and saw the roses were from her husband. He wrote on the note: I'm sorry we argued last night. This should make you feel better. Love, Hugh.

Bonnie stood up, picked up the vases with the roses and brought them to another co-worker down the hall and put them on the stunned woman's desk. "This is my way of saying I appreciate you," and walked back to her office.

******

Giving a gift needs to have no expectations attached. If there are, that greatly diminishes the value of the gift. You do not want to do this. If you take the time to carefully consider a gift that will be meaningful to them and not expect anything in return, your spouse's heart will be touched. It doesn't need to be an expensive gift, but the more thought put into it, the more valuable it becomes. For instance, if your spouse likes daisies, you could get them a bunch of them, or a picture with daisies, perhaps some clothing with daisies, a daisy cookie; the list is infinite.

Do you know that the best gift you can give your spouse is yourself? Your time and attention are greatly appreciated and cherished. Spending time together will enrich your relationship. The walks along the beach, kicking stones, splashing in the water, and talking while sitting in the sand creates a wonderful memory for you both.

Creating a delicious meal together is also a fun and tasty gift you can give. Purchasing food that is not on your normal grocery list could be an exciting and exhilarating time. Dinner by candlelight would also be a sensuous gift that you could easily set up. Have soft music playing in the background. This is an excellent experiential gift that will be greatly loved by your spouse.

When you were a child, perhaps you picked flowers for your mother and gave them to her. You had a real feeling of accomplishment. You could see by her response that she loved the thoughtful gift. You chose each flower carefully and arranged them perfectly. Maybe you drew a picture for her, and she put it on the refrigerator. That was a prominent spot for all to see the picture you drew and showed she was proud of it. This is the same kind of gift that your spouse will appreciate. Your spouse wants to be thought of by you. These types of gifts show that you are thinking of them.

What was your favorite gift that you received that really touched your heart? More than likely, it had more to do with the thought behind it than the actual monetary value of the gift. It's the gifts that say, "I love you," "I appreciate you," and "You are special," that make a difference in the way you feel about yourself and your spouse.

Say "I'm sorry" with a gift

However, if you have had a fight with your spouse, or made a mistake, gifts may help in the reconciliation process. A nice gift shows the sincerity of the apology and conveys the message that you are interested in working the problem out and being unified once more. A nice note or card with this would be appropriate to convey your feelings on the matter unlike the cold calculating message from the husband that sent his wife roses in the illustration at the beginning of this chapter.

Special gifts from the heart

I have heard of one loving husband that wanted to give his wife a much-needed gift ... a night in a hotel to have some quiet time and pampering just for her. This would include dining, hot tub, and other pampering measures. The wife was faithful in serving her family and working outside of the home. The husband appreciated all that she did that he wanted to give her something special and just for her to enjoy. A little quiet time away can be so refreshing. The husband knew what his wife would like and took steps to put something special together for her. Needless to say, the wife was so surprised and excited about taking her day away. The impact on the wife of her husband's gift to her greatly warmed her heart. She was drawn closer to him.

Study your spouse to know what they would really like. Write down some action steps to make it happen, and then follow through on them. Surprise them with your thoughtfulness. You will see how touched they are and their love for you will shine. They may have never been treated like this in their life, so it means a lot and helps them grow in self-confidence and in their commitment to you.

You will add value to your marriage by giving gifts of love to your spouse. It will create a wonderful and romantic relationship between you two and show the importance of the marriage. Your spouse is a gift from God. He thought about who to create for you and what all the blessings would be for you. They are a gift from the heart of the Lord, who knows how to give the best gifts.

May God bless your home, and keep your marriage ... in Jesus' name, Amen.

Chapter 8: If You're Happy and You Know It – Smile

It's always nice to have someone in your life who can make you smile even when they're not around.

- Unknown

There's a childhood song that goes, "If you're happy and you know it, clap your hands." Then it would say to stomp your feet, say amen, and then do all three. The main goal of the exercise was to show you were happy. Communicating happiness is important in a marriage as it is anywhere else, such as work, or other interactions with people. If you don't show that you are happy, the assumption is that you are sad or mad. I believe people can be perfectly happy without showing it, but what could be the importance of showing it?

Communication is more than words; it's also body language. You sometimes can receive more of a message from the language they are showing with their body, than the actual words. If your arms are crossed, what message does that give? The other person may interpret it as being closed off and not open to discussion. Hands on hips may show aggression. No smile may indicate boredom or anger. There is no misunderstanding if a person smiles. Happiness and contentment are shown through a smile. A large smile may indicate that the person is thrilled. There is power in a smile. It can make another person smile (or at least encourage them to).

Seeing a smile encourages us. If someone is happy, then you can be happy, too. It is contagious to smile. So you as a married couple are able to encourage each other with smiling. If you smile at each other, you are sending a message that you are happy with the one you have married. You are thrilled to be a part of their life. They make your heart feel good. Seeing them makes your day. Do you smile just at the thought of your spouse? They don't even have to be in the same room. The many ways they have touched your heart makes you feel so good that you can't help but smile.

Helping your spouse smile

In helping your spouse smile, you are showing them how much you love and care for them. Being happy and smiling are so good for a marriage. It represents the joy you feel together. However, there are some days that just aren't that great. Your spouse comes home after a bad day of work, and they are in a rotten mood. This is your cue to help them relax and get in a better mood.

You could meet them at the door with a smile showing how happy you are to see them. Even if they don't return the smile, know that you are on the right track. Allow them to talk about their day and listen attentively. Listening to them is very valuable, even if you are not able to fix the problem. After they have wound down a bit and relaxed, then you can think of a way to make them smile by either telling a joke, tickling them, being over dramatic in showing your love for them by being silly and kissing them all over their face. If you find, they still are not in the mood for this type of banter, allow them to just relax for the evening. Be attentive, but maybe they just need a little space. Offer to take them out for the evening to forget their day. That might bring a smile on their face.

You could try singing to them the song "Smile" that starts out, "Smile, though your heart is aching, smile, even though it's breaking..." It is a song sure to bring a smile and encourage their heart. You can hold them in your arms, sway back and forth, and sing to them. Perhaps, if able, add a dip into the dance. It's hard not to smile when you've been dipped.

Complement them

Let your spouse know that they have a beautiful smile. Tell them how much you love to see it and how it makes you feel when you do see their smile. Perhaps they have just had their hair done, or shaved, or made some other change to their appearance. Notice it and complement them on it. It is sure to bring a smile. Perhaps the change they made turns you on sexually. Let them be aware of that in your own way.

Show those pearly whites

Smiling is good for the soul; it lowers blood pressure and lightens moods. Be prepared to always give your best smile. You never know when someone will need it … especially your spouse. If you want to show someone you care about them … smile. This says a lot more than words for it comes from the heart.

The Lord smiles upon us and shows us his favor. His smile tells us of his great love for us. Just as we smile on children, God smiles on us.

May God bless your home, and keep your marriage ... in Jesus' name, Amen.

Chapter 9: Appropriate Touch

Sexual touching is important in any growing relationship; however, it should not be the only time a couple touches.

- Dr. Kevin Leman, author of Sex Begins in the Kitchen

Touching someone can be healing. Perhaps that's why many times Jesus would touch someone to heal them. Touch isn't only healing physically, but emotionally, if done correctly. So many people are scarred in their soul from physical abuse, that a touch made on them that reminds them of the abuse could make them fearful and cause them to retract from you. This is true for both children and adults. The key is sensitivity to what they may have experienced in their life.

In marriage, your spouse may or may not have had an abusive experience, but it is still wise to be sensitive on how you touch them. You probably have learned how your spouse likes to be touched and how they don't. If they seem distant when you touch them, that is probably an indication that they don't like it. When it comes to sexual touching, it is appropriate to talk about what each of you likes and feels comfortable with in making contact. If they do not like something that you do like, love and respect them enough not to do it. This will bring you closer together. Touching your spouse is encouraged in the Bible.

"... a lovely deer, a graceful doe. Let her breasts fill you at all times with delight; be intoxicated always in her love,"[7] (Proverbs 5:19).

Maybe you can give your spouse a treat by rubbing them with massage oil or lotion. This will help them relax and feel loved. Purchasing a nice-smelling oil will work wonders using aromatherapy on a harried heart. It will feel so good to your spouse to have their body rubbed. Read up on some massage techniques in which you can surprise them. They will appreciate all your effort. "Research by Tiffany Field of the Touch Research Institute in Miami has found that a mas- sage from a loved one can not only ease pain but also soothe depression and strengthen a relationship."[8]

Other important touches

Holding hands is not just for dating ... it's forever. If your spouse holds your hand, what message does that communicate to you? Does it say that they love, support, and value you? Intertwining fingers gives a stronger message. It feels closer and gives the feeling that your spouse doesn't want to lose you. You can hold hands just about anywhere. It is perfectly acceptable in public and may make people give a little sigh and smile when they see you both holding hands. It gives a good message of a sturdy relationship.

What about a game of footsie? This is done usually with the legs of two people intertwining and rubbing each other up and down the leg. It can be very fun at a formal dinner with the tablecloth covering the legs and you both are trying to act like nothing is happening. Only you two know what is going on under the table. You may both be relaxing at home reading a book on each end of

---

[7] *The Holy Bible: English Standard Version.* (Pr 5:19), (Wheaton: Standard Bible Society 2001).

[8] Carey Benedict, N.P. Web,

http://www.nytimes.com/2010/02/23/health/23mind.html (21 Jun 2013).

the couch where a little footsie is possible. Here's a web link on how to play footsie: http://www.wikihow.com/Play-Footsie

Being gentle in touching your spouse is important. It shows that you value them and don't want to scare them off. A soft touch to the side of the face is very endearing, hugs feel protective, and light kisses are just nice.

The blessing of touch

In biblical times, touch was part of the action taken when one was blessing another. For example, parents brought their children to Jesus so that he could lay his hand on them and bless them. Also, when Jacob received the blessing rather than Esau from their father, Isaac, it was important that he laid his hand on them. Interesting that in the future, when Jacob blessed Joseph's sons, Joseph placed his father's hands on the heads of the two boys, and Jacob switched his hands. "He put Ephraim on his right side and Manasseh on his left. (So Ephraim was near Israel's left hand, and Manasseh was near Israel's right hand.) Joseph brought the boys close to Israel. But Israel crossed his arms and put his right hand on the head of Ephraim, who was younger. He put his left hand on the head of Manasseh, the firstborn son."[9] There is something powerful in the family context of being blessed by those that they love.

Your spouse needs your blessing. Touch them and pray over them daily and watch for God's goodness in both of your lives.

May God bless your home, and keep your marriage ... in Jesus' name, Amen.

Chapter 10: Communicate Your Dreams and Future

Dialoging about the future with your love interest requires you to be open and honest about your feelings, thoughts, and concepts.

- Marvin Sapp, from his book, I Win

What did you dream you wanted to do when you were young? Perhaps you wanted to be a doctor, fireman or actor and would pretend to be that person for fun. As you grow older, those dreams may change somewhat, but they are shaping you into the person God has meant for you to be. There is a passion in your heart to follow a road paved just for you. Now that you are married, your dreams and your spouse's dreams need to work together. They can if there is good communication.

Hopefully, you started these conversations before you became married, but if not, that's okay. It's never too late to communicate. Knowing your spouse's dreams tells you a lot about who they are and what they hope for in life. It will give you help in knowing how to support your spouse.

Ways to communicate

Asking the right questions can help facilitate the communication of dreams for the future. They need to be open-ended to receive more information. If the answer is a simple yes or no, that leaves a lot of room for speculation. The questions need to allow your spouse to think for a bit before answering. Here are some examples of questions you can ask:

- If you could be anything in the world you wanted with no barriers present, what would you be and why?

- What passion has God put on your heart and how has that developed in you?

- In what ways do you feel you are missing out on your development?

- How can I support you in growing in your passion?

- How did you grow in your passion today?

- What opportunities do you feel like you missed today?

- Where would you love to be doing in five years' time?

There are, of course, many other questions that you can ask, but hopefully, this gets you started. It's most important just to get the dialogue started and keep it going. Each day can bring new insights on the direction we are to travel. Don't miss an opportunity to share in these new insights. They are valuable tools to use as you grow together in your marriage.

Ways to support your spouse and their dream

Once you understand your spouse's dream for the future, there are ways that you can support them in meeting this dream. It's important to keep the dream in front of both of you, so that you can see the improvement on getting closer to the goal. Please understand that both of your dreams are valid and should be equally supported.

Ask them regularly about how they are doing regarding fulfilling their dream. Knowing that you want to talk to them about it and that it's on your mind will encourage your spouse. They will feel confident in pursuing the dream knowing that you support them.

Give little gifts that represent their dream. This will touch their heart knowing that you were thoughtful enough to think of them and their dream. For example, if they want to be a teacher, giving them a gift to encourage them in their pursuit such as a book on learning styles, or maybe an apple ornament for the Christmas tree, will go a long way for them.

Help them get the education they need to fulfill their dream. Maybe there are courses available on-line or nearby that could meet the requirements for the degree they may need. Scholarships are usually available for many different careers, so helping to find those resources would be a huge assistance to them.

If they are taking classes to get a degree, it would be helpful if you could support them by doing more of the housework, cooking, or shopping, or taking care of the kids. Supporting your spouse as they work on fulfilling their dream is valuable and can be done in many ways.

Send encouraging notes to them. Let them know you are proud of them in their pursuit of going after their dream. These notes will give them a boost of confidence … even on the hardest days. This will show them how much you love and support them bringing you both closer together.

Helping your spouse fulfill their dream will be a gift that will bless both of you as you work together to be all you were meant to be. "I press on toward the goal for the prize of the upward call of God in Christ Jesus." May these words help you to press on to what God has in store for you.

May God bless your home, and keep your marriage … in Jesus' name, Amen.

Chapter 11: Do You Have a Special Couple Song?

You didn't learn how to play an instrument well in one night. It will take time to learn how to "make music" with your spouse too.

- J & G Murphy

Nora looked in the cupboards. All the dishes were put in the wrong place. I wish Dan wouldn't help; she thought as she began to take the dishes out.

Dan came in from outside and saw her taking the dishes out. "Hey, I just rearranged that cupboard."

"I know. Now I am putting it back the right way."

"Who says which way is the right way?"

"Oh, I suppose you have a lot of experience with dishes and kitchen set up."

******

Knowing how to live life with your spouse in a manner that is pleasing to you both takes work. It's not something that comes naturally, no matter how good you got along on your dates; there's something totally different in living under the same roof. You learn a lot more about each other, because you see more of them and learn their true personality and moods.

In learning to live together, you will see that there is a reaction to every action. It's like learning to dance together. Ballroom dancing requires the dancers to know each other's moves as they float across the floor, or else it may look more like clogging. To move smoothly through your marriage together, it takes time, patience, and a lot of understanding. It's give and take where you are willing to give a lot to your spouse and vice versa. Giving is where the blessing is … that's where the music is heard. It's a love song inside the heart that sings joyfully as you both give to the other. Luke wrote in Acts 20:35, "In all things I have shown you that by working hard in this way we must help the weak and remember the words of the Lord Jesus, how he himself said, 'It is more blessed to give than to receive.'"[9]

Love more than you ever did before

There are going to be times when you quite frankly get on each other's nerves. You will want to redecorate the living room one way and your spouse the other. One will want a man cave and the other a sewing room. Personalities begin to clash as each has their own idea of what home should be like. Harsh words may be said before you or your spouse realizes they left your mouth. This person who just weeks ago was the most perfect person for you suddenly doesn't seem so perfect … in fact, they sometimes seem like the wrong person.

I want to assure you that these feelings are natural. Most couples experience this at the beginning, and sometimes further into their

marriage. You wonder what happened to the unconditional love you felt for your spouse, or their love for you. Now it feels conditional.

Communication really is the key to work through this. Remember the sweet manner you handled each other before being married. Get some of that back by intentionally showing love and respect to your spouse, no matter what the situation is, and always have the goal of working it out. Don't be ready to flee

---

[9] *The Holy Bible: English Standard Version,* (Ac 20:35), (Wheaton: Standard Bible Society, 2001)

when things get tough; there's no maturing with that. Always be willing to talk and work out any misunderstandings or disagreements. That is where courage shows in an individual. You are willing to work hard to make this marriage work. That is God-honoring, and he will help you make it through.

Love your spouse each day like it's the last day you will have together. That kind of love gets your attention, and you realize that whatever it is you are not agreeing on has no comparison to the love you feel for each other.

As the years go by, you will have learned so much about your spouse that you will start finishing each other's sentences. You will feel comfortable together and truly want to help each other reach their goals in life. This type of giving is heartfelt and each of you will realize that the one they chose to wed was the perfect choice for them. It just takes a bit of time and grit to get there. But as you float across the floor in your understanding of each other, you will see the wonderful gift God has given you in your spouse. Praise God for his infinite wisdom in bringing you both together and for providing for your both through the years.

Lovemaking

When it comes to making love with your spouse, the closeness you experience is meant for just you two. Learning and enjoying each other's bodies is part of the process in growing in marriage. It may take a bit of time to get the rhythm that is satisfying for you both, but don't get discouraged, you will get there. If you are both patient and loving during this time, as well as communicating, sex will be an enjoyable and blessed time that you will both grow into and perhaps become more creative as the years go by.

Making music with your spouse is all about learning life together along with the give and take married couples need to do for each other. As time goes by, you will both be growing in unity, not being each other's puppets, but honoring the Lord with your life together.

May God bless your home, and keep your marriage ... in Jesus' name, Amen

Chapter 12: What Can You Give?

Love is the greatest gift when given. It is the highest honor when received.

- Fawn Weaver

Think about the best gift you have ever received. What are the reasons that it was the best? It could have been because of the person it came from, how it met a great need in your life, or just the thought that went into getting it for you. I'm sure there are many other possible reasons that it was the best, but when you think of it, your heart warms and your mind goes back to the moment of receiving it. You will never forget it.

Now consider the ways you can give "gifts" to your spouse every day. It doesn't have to be bought, but maybe just a little thought put into it. For example, an encouraging note found in a lunch bag lets your spouse know that you are thinking of them. It will be appreciated and make their day better. Using the reasons behind the best gift you received, create a similar feeling for your spouse. It may be a simple gift such as washing the dishes, but if your spouse has had a rough day, this gift could be well received.

It is many times the experience that is the best gift. You could take your spouse out for ice cream, go fishing, lay on the beach, take a bike ride, or travel someplace special. These extraordinary trips are meaningful and will be remembered by your mate. It doesn't need to be something planned, it can be spur of the moment ... and sometimes that is better.

Giving your love

The most precious gift you can give your mate is your love. You may think, "What do you mean? I love my mate already." Let me clarify for you what is meant by giving your love. Let's look at the Scriptures and find out how God loves. We know of the great sacrifice he has given us through his son, Jesus. Jesus suffered at the hands of people he was trying to save, nailed to a cross and died. He didn't have to do this but chose to because of his great love for us. He gave it all. While giving it all like Jesus did may seem a bit radical to you in present day Christianity, don't let that stop you from investigating how you can give it all for your spouse. Can you love like Jesus? What we show to our mate reflects how we feel about God. T.P. Crosby wrote in his commentary *Opening Up 2 and 3 John*, "Loving one another is not only an imitation of God's love to us; it is also an outward expression of our inward love for God."[10]

Love and trust

Love and trust are closely related. If you truly love your spouse, you should be able to fully trust them. When you can trust someone totally knowing that they love you completely and unconditionally, you will be able to surrender everything to them. "I Surrender All" is a tough hymn to sing in all truthfulness. When have you surrendered everything to anyone?

Is there any area where you don't trust your mate? Ask yourself why you feel this way. Then determine what needs to happen before you can trust them fully. Talk to your spouse about it and find a way to be able to trust each other more. Contact a Christian marriage counselor, if needed, to help you pursue this. You will both feel be glad you did.

---

[10] Crosby . *Opening up 2 and 3 John*. Opening Up Commentary (Le- ominster: Day One Publications, 2006), 32.

Need control?

Do you feel like you need control over the relationship? You were born with a "that's mine" mentality in your nature and you simply don't like to give up anything. Control feels safe to most people. You can allow yourself to be deceived thinking you have control over everything in your life, but the truth is you don't. Life can take a serious turn at any moment. The only true thing we must hold unto is Jesus.

Trying to control your spouse is not realistic, and frankly, it's not healthy. Your relationship is not based on control, but on love. Letting go of control will show your mate how much you love them. You were both created for the other one as helpers, not as controllers. You are to work together to support one another through life.

The only area of control you are given is self-control. Not many are great at controlling themselves as shown in 1 Corinthians 7:5, "...so that Satan may not tempt you because of your lack of self-control."[11] However, you are able to seek God to help you with this spiritual fruit (Galatians 5:22-23). The more of any spiritual fruit that you have will enable you to show more love to your spouse. This is an important aspect of having a happy marriage.

May God bless your home, and keep your marriage ... in Jesus' name, Amen.

---

[11] *The Holy Bible: English Standard Version,* (1 Corinthians 7:5), (Wheaton: Standard Bible Society, 2001).

Chapter 13: What's So Funny?

The more things we can laugh about, the more alive we become:
The more things we can laugh about together, the more connected
we become.

- Frank Pittman

Tracy quietly tiptoes around the corner of the house. She has the remote in her hand.

Brad pulls into the driveway and from his remote has the garage door begin to rise.

Tracy pushes the button and giggles. The door comes back down before he reaches it with the car. She can see the confused look on his face, which makes her giggle more.

He tries to put the door up again, and Tracy brings it back down.

Brad gets out of the car and walks up to the garage door and checks to see if there is a loose wire or if it is off-track.

Just as he walks back to the car, Tracy put the door up. This time Brad sees her.

He chases her around the house and they both fall on the grass laughing.

"So, it's Tricky Tracy up to her ol' antics. We'll I know what to do with tricksters like you." He begins to tickle her.

She cries out for mercy, and he stops. They love to laugh together.

******

When you remember the best times of your life, was laughter included in those memories? Often, when you look back, you remember sharing a good hearty laugh with people you love and wish for those moments to come again. Laughter makes you feel so good … and it is so good for you.

There are numerous health benefits to laughter including the lowering of blood pressure, it's a great work out for your abs, it helps cells fight against tumors, it makes you more alert and creative, and improves memory. These reasons alone are enough to want to laugh on a regular basis. Knowing these benefits and the fun it is to laugh should make you want to help your spouse to laugh more. Because of the love you have for them, sharing in laughing is not only helping them health-wise, but in your relationship with them, because you are creating great memories together.

Secret laughter

Have you ever had a time when you and your spouse shared something that was hilarious? Every now and then, you just say a word or have a look that relates to that incident and you both laugh all over again. Everyone else has no idea why you are laughing, but that's okay. The connection you have with your mate in remembering something funny gives you a special bond.

Does God laugh?

Have you ever wondered if God laughed? Does he have a sense of humor or is he pursed-lipped like sourpuss Christians can sometimes be? The Bible tells you that God created laughter (Genesis 21:6), so you can imagine that he also partakes in it from time to time. Just reading the Scriptures sometimes will make you chuckle at the funny ways people respond to God, and then how he responds back. It's very funny material. For instance, when Moses was up the mountain talking to the Lord and getting the Ten Commandments, the people below were running amok. Aaron, the priest, decides to keep peace in the camp by making an idol for the people to worship since they are getting restless. He collects gold and carefully crafts the calf and presents it to the Israelite people as their god who rescued them from Egypt. The people go wild and start worshiping the calf through sexual acts.

God knows what is going on and tells Moses to go back down to get control over the people. When he walks down with the Ten Commandments and sees the vulgarity of the people, he throws both tablets down on the ground where they break, melts the calf, and make the people drink the melted god. He then goes to Aaron and asked why this happened. Aaron starts backstroking and says, "I said to them, 'Let any who have gold take it off.' So they gave it to me, and I threw it into the fire, and out came this calf."[12] He was acting like it wasn't his fault at all. In fact, he makes it look like he hardly had anything to do with it. Human nature is funny.

How to share funny moments

People can be so funny. Maybe go with your spouse to a public place just to people watch. Quirks come out naturally. Humans are created so uniquely that they can be very funny. Such as the woman who always digs back to the last item on a shelf in the grocery store to make sure it is the least touched item. Not normal. People with animals are a lot of fun to watch. You never know what animals will do … just like kids … and their innocence and enthusiasm can give laughs to those watching.

You could take your spouse to a comedy and enjoy the laughs together. Movies, plays or perhaps a stand-up comedian (be careful about the type of material they have … could be vulgar), can make for an enjoyable evening with the one you love.

---

[12] *The Holy Bible: English Standard Version,* (Exodus 32:24). (Wheaton: Standard Bible Society, 2001).

You can be funny

Discover your funny bone and act up a bit. Silly antics make light of a situation and bring a smile to the face of your mate. Dressing in silly clothes can be funny along with comedic actions. Have fun being a clown every now and then. Not only will you enjoy it, but your spouse will always remember it about you and how you made them laugh.

May God bless your home, and keep your marriage ... in Jesus' name, Amen.

Chapter 14: Communicate Through the Written Word

The instant communication tools of today have nearly obliterated the love letter, which is a crying shame.

- Joshua Gordon

She opens the envelope. Inside is a card with a picture of a bee on the front. *Why would he send me a card with a bee?* Looking inside the card, she began to read the note. "To my dear wife, I love you more than anything and want you to 'bee' all that you can 'bee.' You have my unending support."

******

As written earlier, communication is so important in a marriage, and finding different ways of communicating to one another is beneficial. One way that touches the heart is the writing of notes and letters. Remember as a child when someone would write you a special note and attempt to pass it to you without the teacher seeing? You couldn't wait until you opened it up and read the words written just for you. It meant something to you.

Now that you are older and married, the thrill of receiving a note written just for you is still there. I'm sure your spouse also loves to receive special notes. Who wouldn't? It is a tangible way of showing how much you care for the other person in words constructed by you. You take more time to write a note or letter, for you want to make sure you are using just the right word in describing your feelings for the other person.

Ronald Reagan wrote beautiful letters to his wife, Nancy. They were all kept by her over the years. She knew that he loved her with all his heart. They were written for her to read again and again. That's the nice thing about letters and notes; they last a very long time. The feelings you have for your spouse can be documented in a beautiful way through writing them in a loving letter.

God's model

Love letters are God's specialty. He wrote you all about how he feels about you in the Bible. His love is described in so many forms of writing in both the Old and New Testament. His love never changes, but the ways he can tell you about how he feels are numerous. From the very beginning, he loved Adam and Eve, and even though they sinned, he still provided for them. That begins a pattern of loving many sinful children afterward, including you. However, he found many ways to express his love to you by writing down his laws to protect you. He used prophets in the Old Testament to show the Messiah was coming. Jeremiah 29:11 states, "For I know the plans I have for you, declares the LORD, plans for welfare and not for evil, to give you a future and a hope."[13] It is important to God to show how he feels about you and what he can do to help you.

These are the same kind of reasons that you could write your heart on paper and deliver the words to your spouse. Not only will it do good for your spouse's heart, but also yours as you process your feelings to be able to write them down. You know you love your spouse, but perhaps you may discover a greater depth of that love by writing love letters to him or her. As any writer

---

[13] *The Holy Bible: English Standard Version*, (Jeremiah 29:11), (Wheaton: Standard Bible Society, 2001).

can tell you, when they sit down to write, something pours out of them from deep inside. It cannot be controlled for a writer must write what comes out. The same is true with a person in love. Love is so deep seeded that you cannot help expressing it in words that describe your feelings.

Writing the letter

Find a time by yourself to write the letter. If you can find some nice stationary, that's a plus, but if you can't, that's okay … use what you have. If you want some inspiration in writing, read Song of Solomon, that should get you started.

Begin by thinking of all the attributes your spouse has that you love. Choose one to write about, because you want to save some for future letters. Explain how that characteristic impacts you and your feelings about them. Encourage them by telling them how much they mean to you. Express your joy in having them in your life and what it has meant to you.

You could write about a time you remember fondly about them and how it made you feel. Perhaps you were on a date, sharing in ministry, special times with children, there are a lot of times you could use for your letters. Seeing that you remember them will make your spouse feel special. You could start out with remembering your wedding and all the special things that happened that day.

Special Delivery

Now how should you deliver the letter? Be creative. Maybe putting it on their pillow, in a lunch bag as they leave for work, slip it into their coat pocket, mail it, in their drawer, and so on. When they find it, it will be special surprise for them. These thoughtful letters will be treasured for years to come. Why not try it today?

May God bless your home, and keep your marriage … in Jesus' name, Amen.

Chapter 15: Can You Guess What They Like to Do? Just Do It.

A great spouse loves you exact the way you are. An ex- traordinary spouse helps you grow; inspires you to be, do and give your very best.

- Fawn Weaver

The box laying on her bed is large and has the look of extravagance with its red velvet bow. She opens the box and sees a lovely red and black dress neatly folded. She picks it up and holds it up to herself seeing that it fit perfectly.

Her husband was so thoughtful in buying the dress as an encouragement to her. She was beginning her new job, and the colors matched the company's colors. Her heart was touched. He knew what she would like and went ahead and did it. The good thought turned into action. That's the formula of a successful deed.

******

There is nothing like having the support of a spouse, especially when changes in life occur. New challenges such as a new job or new baby, or it could be a different type of challenge such as cancer or caring for a loved one during their illness. Life brings on many different occurrences, and while they all have a purpose, it's good to know that you are supported greatly by your spouse. What if your spouse is going through a weight-loss program? This can be a touchy subject, but if handled correctly, with sensitivity and grace, you could help your spouse through the challenge by encouraging them along the way. They are working hard at changing an eating habit, and if you ignore it, or worse put them down, it can create devastating results in your relationship. However, if you are a team player and help them by eating what they are eating, exercising with them, telling them how great they are doing, and assure them of your love for them just as they are. When you can see differences, tell them, and celebrate with them. This will lead them to the road of success and help them overcome the obstacles they come up against, because you are there in the trenches with them, loving them completely.

You want that kind of support too when you are going through a new journey in life. That constant support from your spouse will work wonders. Appreciate all that your spouse does to show your support.

Jesus showed love and support

They had purpose. In helping his disciples become everything they were meant to be, Jesus made sure that they were encouraged and equipped to grow. He would sit down at times only with his disciples to teach things he wanted them to know. He did this at the Sermon on the Mount (Matthew 5). It was a special time just for them to hear Jesus's instruction. He begins to tell them how to really be happy (the Beatitudes), which is quite different than what the world says is happiness. Their emotional health was important to Jesus, because of his love for them. Likewise, you as a spouse can show the importance of your mate being happy. You love them and you want them to experience joy.

The Last Supper (Matthew 26) was also a very intimate time for Jesus and his disciples. He was expressing through the bread and cup the great sacrifice he would be making for them. He knew life was going to change very quickly that night, and he wanted them to be as prepared as possible. He had been telling them that he would die and rise again in three days. They didn't understand, but he told them anyway so that they could remember after he died so they could have hope.

Hope is a wonderful gift to give someone you love. You could help your spouse's hopes and dreams come alive. By your words and actions, you can help them believe in themselves … that they can do it. Help them to be as equipped as possible. Is it something new they need to learn? Help them study (you could learn something, too). Schedule conflicts often hamper the steps of following a dream. If the kids need transportation to soccer practice, here's your opportunity to step up. Be the hero to your spouse.

In giving of yourself, that will make the biggest impact on your mate to show them how much you love and adore them. The respect you show for the endeavor they are doing will long live in their hearts. Just like Jesus knew when giving of himself to his disciples.

May God bless your home, and keep your marriage … in Jesus' name, Amen.

Chapter 16: Active Listening

The goal in marriage is not to think alike, but to think together.

- Robert C. Dodds

"Can you hear me now?" This question was asked by Verizon to show the importance of taking steps to being able to hear well. In fact, it was a part of their marketing to show they had the best equipment and service that would give clear communication and lessen technical difficulties such as dropped calls. Sometimes when you communicate with a spouse, it may feel like the call has been dropped, because of the issue of not actively listening to your spouse.

Communication skills are needed to have the most effectively engaged marriage partnership, where both individuals can clearly understand the other. This is not an easy task, but one that continually needs work. Not wanting to do the work is where most couples suffer in their relationships for the communication is not good. When this breaks down, each person has only their instincts to rely on in discerning their spouse's needs and desires. Most times, an individual will discern with their own life experience, because that is all they must use. By doing this, faulty thinking patterns may get into the process and a wrong message is received.

Steps for active listening

1. Take the time to listen. When your spouse wants to talk to you, stop what you are doing and give them your full attention.

2. Give non-verbal signals that you are interested in what they are saying. Make eye contact, nod to show understanding, and lean in a bit to show you are listening.

3. Ask clarifying questions. Paraphrase what they said in a question form, such as, "I hear you say ... Is this correct?" If it isn't, allow them to explain further.

4. Ask if there is any more they would like to share with you.

5. Thank them for communicating with you. Give feedback upon what you heard and be sensitive to their feelings, also reading their body language for emotional indicators.

Using these steps will enhance your marriage, for the effort you are putting into listening to your spouse will show how much you love them. Jesus said in Revelation to each of the churches he was addressing, "Everyone who has ears should listen to what the Spirit says to the churches."[14] The churches could show their love for Jesus by listening to what his Spirit said and obey it. It means a lot to him. He doesn't want the churches to be unengaged into his mission. He loves them and wants them to join him in what he is doing. It's the same thing with being married. We want our mate to be involved in what we are doing because we love them. Good listening will allow for that to happen. When you first start working with the steps, it may feel stilted, but that's okay, as you practice it will become more natural in your communication with the spouse.

Loving your spouse through listening

Listening to your spouse intently as they share their heart with you is one of the best ways you can show them that you love them. I am sure you have had

_____

[14] *The Everyday Bible: New Century Version,* (Revelation 3:6), Nashville, TN: Thomas Nelson, Inc. (2005)

the experience of someone who asks, "How are you?" but doesn't stop to hear your response. Research shows that people only really hear 25 to 50 percent of what is said. That is a lot of missed information. That's why there are so many misunderstandings in the world. People won't take the time to really listen.

God promises to listen to you even when you don't have the words to pray. In Romans 8:26 is written, "Likewise the Spirit helps us in our weakness; for we do not know how to pray as we ought, but that very Spirit intercedes with sighs too deep for words.[15] Whatever it is, God wants to listen to you. In that same spirit, truly listen to your spouse. This will be a wonderful loving gift that you can give them.

May God bless your home, and keep your marriage ... in Jesus' name, Amen.

---

[15] *The Holy Bible: New Revised Standard Version,* (Romans 8:26), (Nashville: Thomas Nelson Publishers 1989)

Chapter 17: Build Them Up

*The highest love a person can have for you is to wish
you to evolve into the best person you can be.*

- David Viscott

When building a pizza, many believe that the more ingredients on it, the better. So you start with the dough and sauce, this is pretty plain. Maybe throw on some cheese which makes it better. Then you choose other items such as pepperoni, sausage, olives, mushrooms, green pepper, and pineapple. Now this is a pizza to enjoy and share with others. It took your initiative to make it better. It wouldn't happen on its own.

Building your spouse takes initiative, too. You add the ingredients into your spouse's life that will make them better, which will not only bless them, but others. Your love for them will be evident in the effort you put forth in helping them to grow. This is a sacrifice of time and energy on your part, but it will be wisely invested in your mate.

How to support your spouse

Using words and actions, you can encourage your spouse and build them up. Use words that have a positive tone rather than negative. You are not there to tear them down. They may fail at what they do, but you have also failed from time to time. Failing at something is a wonderful teacher. The lessons learned help an individual succeed the next time. Do not condemn them in any way for a nonachievement. It may be tempting to say something like, "Remember when you ..." recalling a past failure, but don't do it. That will only create a divide between the two of you. Show unconditional love and encouragement towards them.

When they fail, be there to support them. Give hugs when needed. Talk to them about their experience and what they have gained from it. Encourage them to try again if it seems appropriate. Assure them of your love for them and how you are proud of them for trying. Ask if there's anything you can do to help them. They will appreciate your sincere heart.

God has great plans for your mate, as well as for you, and part of that plan is putting the two of you together to encourage and help one another in building each other up to experience all that the Lord has planned for you both. It was not by coincidence that the two of you met and fell in love. There are special gifts that you both have that will enhance the life journey of the other. You are both helpers to each other.

Every day, find what it is that your spouse needs to help them grow. Help them as much as you can for that investment will payback great returns in your life together. Join their vision, as you allow them to join your vision, and work together to reach the goals set before you.

Pray for your spouse daily for them to grow in Christ and continually seek him for all their needs. Ask your mate for specific prayer requests and make note of them. Pray on these requests every day. Putting your spiritual energy into their success is beautiful that will stay in their heart forever. Plus, it works. Prayer is the most powerful thing you can do for your spouse. Don't neglect to lift the love of your life to the one who created them.

Another great thing about prayer is that you can do it together as a couple. Not only does this bring you both into the throne room of God together, but it also gives you a glimpse deep into their soul which you may not have seen before.

Here's an example written by E.A. Blum in *The Bible Knowledge Commentary: An Exposition of the Scriptures*, "The command is new in that it is a special love for other believers based on the sacrificial love of Jesus: As I have loved you, so you must love one another. Christians' love and support for one another enable them to survive in a hostile world. As Jesus was the embodiment of God's love, so now each disciple should embody Christ's love."[16] The goal here is for you to embody Christ's love. Evaluate how you now do that and find what areas you need to grow in doing this. You basically are being Christ to your mate. Jesus can't hug them now, but he can through you. You are the hands and feet of Jesus. You have opportunity to show how alive he really is by showing his love to your spouse.

May God bless your home, and keep your marriage ... in Jesus' name, Amen.

---

[16] E. A. Blum, John. In J. F. Walvoord & R. B. Zuck (Eds.), *The Bible Knowledge Commentary: An Exposition of the Scriptures* (John 13:34–35), (Wheaton, IL: Victor Books 1985).

Chapter 18: Relinquish Your Rights

A fool in love makes no sense to me. I only think you are a fool if you do not love.

- Unknown

"It's my right!"

You may have heard this said or perhaps said it yourself. You feel entitled to your inalienable rights as a citizen of your country. While it is true that God has given us rights, and we do need to respect and protect them, it's important to note how Jesus, being God, acted on his rights. He had the right not to be arrested, beaten, and crucified. God, the Father, could have taken him all from that because it wasn't right. Jesus shows that sometimes your rights need to come after the greater good.

In marriage, you both feel the need for respect. Your rights are yours to do with what you want. This means it is a choice to keep your rights or give them away. Being married, there may be a time for you to give up your rights only because of the great love you have for your mate.

Let's think about some of the rights that you do have. You have the right to be a child of God and come to him whenever you have a need in prayer. This is a wonderful right that should be always acted on. You have the right to vote, pay taxes, own property, get paid for work done, and so much more. As a spouse, you have a right to your mate's body as shown in 1 Corinthians 7:3-5. What if your partner is not feeling well, or just not in the mood? Are you going to force your rights on them? If you are a loving mate, the answer would be no, of course not. You would joyfully give up your rights for their betterment. Laying down your life (or your rights) for another … that's Jesus's way.

Giving up your rights does not mean to become a doormat in the marriage. That was never God's plan, but if you can see in each situation what would be the best, not always for you, and sometimes not for either of you, and sometimes when it would just be best for your spouse, that's heartfelt sacrifice … and it will feel so good to you.

Giving up your time

Let's say you have had a busy week at work, and you are looking forward to the weekend for a little rest and relaxation. When you get home, your spouse announces to you that family is coming to visit for the weekend and the house needs to be cleaned. Before you blow a gasket in anticipation of losing your weekend, consider the priority of family. If they are over all the time, maybe you can talk to your mate about rescheduling their visit. However, if you haven't seen them for a while, it is important to keep in touch and share life. There are many dysfunctional families that rarely see each other, so it takes all in- volved to keep family relationships healthy.

While most of the weekend won't be restful, there may be times when you can sneak away for a catnap. Maybe take a lawn chair out- side or climb in a hammock and enjoy the outdoors while you snooze. This will be refreshing for you.

Set a goal for yourself in bonding or learning more about a family member that is coming. You could take them aside and spend some special time together, maybe go fishing, shopping or out to eat in a nice restaurant. Ask open-ended questions that give them opportunities to reveal more of who they are to you. You may be surprised by what you learn. Some people have fascinating histories, but never talk about themselves. Taking time for them to share will be memorable, and your spouse will be very appreciative, too. Find those ways where you can feel good about the situation, so that you can enjoy it as much as your loved one.

You will be blessed by the blessing you give for your mate. Your relationship will blossom by self-giving evidenced in your marriage. Your spouse is a priority to you and showing it will strengthen the marriage and be a model to other married couples who are trying to live together under one roof. It is give and take by both. If both individuals in a marriage decided to give 100% to the other and not 50- 50, you would see wonderful changes in each person that would live to honor the other. This is the picture God gave for marriage. It's a wonderful picture and cannot be compared with any other on earth.

May God bless your home, and keep your marriage ... in Jesus' name, Amen.

Chapter 19: What Do They Need?

The most desired gift of love is not diamonds or roses or chocolate. It is focused attention.

- Rick Warren

A plant of any sort usually needs attention for it to grow. If it doesn't receive the water, light, food, and perhaps conversation needed, it will die. A gardener needs to pay close attention to the needs of the plant. Are the leaves turning yellow? Is it drooping? Are there bugs on them or eating them? Things like this are telltale signs that something is needed for them to survive. If you are not being attentive to plants, they can wither and be no more.

Any living thing needs attention of some sort. Thankfully, you do not need to take care of everything. God does quite a good job at doing that. "Therefore, I tell you, do not worry about your life, what you will eat or what you will drink, or about your body, what you will wear. Is not life more than food, and the body more than clothing? Look at the birds of the air; they neither sow nor reap nor gather into barns, and yet your heavenly Father feeds them. Are you not of more value than they? And can any of you by worrying add a single hour to your span of life? And why do you worry about clothing? Consider the lilies of the field, how they grow; they neither toil nor spin, yet I tell you, even Solomon in all his glory was not clothed like one of these. But if God so clothes the grass of the field, which is alive today and tomorrow is thrown into the oven, will he not much more clothe you—you of little faith? Therefore, do not worry, saying, 'What will we eat?' or 'What will we drink?' or 'What will we wear?'[17] (Matthew 6:25–31)

God already has control over all you need in life, so what does that mean for you in paying attention to your spouse? The verse in Matthew is a model for you in that God loves you so much, he cares about all the details in your life. He doesn't just let you go and fend for yourself. You would probably wither and die if he did.

The details

What do you think are the details in your mate's life that need attention? Are there telltale signs of discouragement, disillusionment, or depression? Their list of needs probably looks pretty like what you need from them. Each person needs to be listened to, appreciated, valued, loved, respected, and nurtured. This has nothing to do with material needs, but more with internal needs. Giving attention to these needs and meeting them will help your spouse grow from the inside out and blossom beautifully.

As a couple, you can practice meeting these needs and growing together. With listening, give them your full attention and response. Let them share how it made them feel. Then allow them to listen to you in the same manner. The same with appreciation. Do you feel appreciated for all you do? In most cases, you probably don't, and as a reflection of that, you probably don't show appreciation to your spouse a lot either. That doesn't mean it has to stay that way. Show heartfelt gratefulness to your spouse. It will make an impact on them, and they will want to do the same for you.

Do you value your spouse like you should? Sometimes you may take them for granted. You wouldn't be the first. What if your house was on fire? What would you grab and run outside with ... and it better not be the X-box. Your spouse is

---

[17] *The Holy Bible: New Revised Standard Version,* (Matthew 6:25– 31), (Nashville: Thomas Nelson Publishers 1989)

valuable and adds worth to your life. The returns are divine! Am I over blowing this issue? Certainly not. Your spouse is worth your all.

These last three, loved, respected, and nurtured, can be combined somewhat for when you truly love someone, you respect them to be who God has planned for them to be. This shows great regard for the person they are, plus you are nurturing them to grow and mature in their spiritual walk discovering who they are and whose they are. God made them an individual and brought you both together for a wonderful purpose. It's in meeting each other's internal needs that will produce a marriage that will soar.

May God bless your home, and keep your marriage ... in Jesus' name, Amen.

Chapter 20: Breakfast in Bed

Marriage is a commitment- a decision to do, all through life, that which will express your love for one's spouse.

-Herman H. Kieval

You fix up the tray just right. There's a single flower in the vase, a perfectly shaped egg that is over easy, lightly toasted bagel, and two strips of bacon. You fold the napkin just right along with putting the silverware and salt and pepper on the tray, and don't forget the brew ... dark roast. You carry the tray to your bedroom, open the door, and lay the tray on the lap of your awaiting spouse. The smile they give you is radiant for you have showed them love that flourish beyond expectation. You didn't have to serve your mate breakfast in bed, but you wanted to show them that they are special to you, so you did.

This is nothing less than the lavished love you experience from God. You cannot deny his love when you get those unexpected favors such as money in the mail that is needed, a call from someone you've been praying for, or healing that comes from a grim prognosis. God's love is evident in the everyday if you look closely for it, but sometimes there are extraordinary factors that play out that go above the level of normal. This is a sign of God's outrageous love for you.

Random Acts

You've probably heard of random acts of kindness. This will be random acts of love. This can be anything from bringing flowers home for your spouse unexpectedly to allowing the football game to be a priority on a Friday night. It's those little special treatments that enrich life, especially for a married couple. Imagine finding one way to surprise your spouse everyday with something they are not expecting. It would be a good exercise for you in being conscious of making the day special for your spouse, as well as building and strengthening your relationship. Remember, these random acts do not need to be big and complex … just thoughtful.

Kind Words and Deeds

Kind hearts are the gardens,

Kind thoughts are the roots,

Kind words are the flowers,

Kind deeds are the fruits.

Take care of your garden,

And keep out the weeds;

Fill it up with sunshine,

Kind words and kind deeds.

—Longfellow[18]

---

[18] P. L. Tan, . *Encyclopedia of 7700 Illustrations: Signs of the Times,* (Garland, TX: Bible Communications, Inc. 1996).

Your marriage is a garden. So many good things come out of it, but it takes work and attention to keep it well maintained. The weeds of life can grow quickly and strangle the good plants growing in your relationship. Those weeds need to be taken out through grace and mercy. Keeping the garden free of weeds is a challenge, but not impossible. It is worth the work put into it. The sunshine you spread in your marriage will allow it to grow in a healthy manner and shine for the world to see.

God's Random Acts of Love

Be aware each day of the random acts of love God does for you. This should inspire you to follow the model given. God blesses you to be a blessing. Are you blessed today with a new inspiration? Are you blessed with abundance today? In any blessing that you are given, find a way to bless another. The person closest to you should be the first person you bless … your spouse. By investing a blessing, you will yield a high return in blessings all to the glory of God.

May God bless your home, and keep your marriage ... in Jesus' name, Amen

Chapter 21: Words are Powerful

I can live for two months on a good compliment.

- Mark Twain

Say what you mean and mean what you say. This wisdom has been used throughout the years and it never gets old. Carefully chosen words can bring about great success, but they can also demolish a kingdom. They can heal the wounds of a broken heart, or they can execute great pain to an individual. Choosing what you say is a direct reflection of who you are from the inside out. If your heart has been scarred and hardened over time, your words will reflect the anguish you feel.

Your words also have a direct impact on your marriage. If you are using words to build up your spouse and help them to see they are valuable, then you are glorifying God with those words and creating a strong bond between you and your spouse. If you have chosen to use words that discourage and create despair, you are breaking down communication and trust in the relationship, and your marriage will suffer. This is not the plan of God for your marriage.

The woman at the well

In John 4, a Samaritan woman arrives at a well; she was hurt and lonely. She felt very unloved by her community, even going to the well for water at the time of day when hardly anyone else would be there. She was used and abused by many men. Her heart was hardened. Day after day she would carry her water jar to the well with her eyes cast downwards hoping that no one would see her, or worse, talk to her.

Then Jesus comes to the well looking for a drink of water. He asks her kindly for a drink. Her response is shock. He talks to her. She's a Samaritan and he a Jew. Suddenly, her world is impacted by him. He treats her with respect. Jesus offers her the living water and takes time to explain it to her. Because of his words to her and the tone, she is drawn to him and wants the living water of which he spoke.

The next words are important. "Jesus said to her, 'Go, call your husband, and come back.'"[19] Why? Because he is helping her become free of the sin she is committing with different men. He is not using words to break her down, but language that lifts her up in a manner. She admits to the sin, and he says, "You are right in saying, 'I have no husband;' for you have had five husbands, and the one you have now is not your husband. What you have said is true!"[20] He is cheering her on as she chooses to take the right path with him. In the following verses, she went away with her head held high to the community that shunned her before and told them about Jesus and how he knew all that she had done. They believed her. Her words were powerful to them. Through Jesus's words, her life was changed, and through her words, others were changed.

This is a great example of how words can change the life of your mate. They may be feeling bad about themselves or circumstances, but your words have

---

[19] *The Holy Bible: New Revised Standard Version.* (John 4:16), (Nashville: Thomas Nelson Publishers 1989).

[20] *The Holy Bible: New Revised Standard Version.* (John 4:17–18), (Nashville: Thomas Nelson Publishers 1989).

the power to possibly change all of that for them, by building them up from the inside out. You treat your spouse with respect and acknowledge the right things they do and say. This is like a healing balm on their heart, just like it was for the Samaritan woman when Jesus spoke to her.

When you think about it, God spoke creation into being. Jesus was described as the "Word" in John. Words written by scholars throughout the centuries still impact people. Words are powerful.

Your own application to this truth

Do you know what words will encourage your spouse? Take some time and brainstorm a list of words that describe your mate. Take those words and expand on them so that you will have an ample supply of spirit building power words in which to bless your mate. For example, your spouse is kind. Think of an example or two of how they are kind. Explain how it affects you when they are kind. Encourage them in their kindness.

Using words to build and power up your marriage will bring you closer together. Words that break down will divide you. Continue in your growing adventure of marriage by being mindful of the words you use, and God will be glorified.

Here are some popular comments that can help your relationship with your spouse:

- I love you.
- I really admire you for... (something specific).
- You know, you might be right.
- What do you need from me, or what can I do for you right now?
- Thank you; I appreciate you.
- I'm sorry; please forgive me.
- You are the most beautiful woman/handsome man in the world.
- You are my best friend.
- Have I told you recently how much I love the way you?

- You rock my world.

Learn to use these words often. It helps...

May God bless your home, and keep your marriage ... in Jesus' name, Amen.

Chapter 22: Missing Their Voice

I dropped a tear in the ocean. The day you find it is the day I will stop missing you.

— Unknown

Military spouses know all about missing their mates. The sacrifice they give to their country is a difficult one. How many of those videos have you seen where the military spouse comes home and surprises either their mate or child? Do you tear up with each one? That shows the heart you must be able to relate to the separation and reunion witnessed.

There are ways they cope with the absence of their loved one. For example, there are pictures around, letters read, perhaps a shirt with their scent on it, and thankfully technologies that help in communication. However, nothing measures up to having that person home and in their arms. Hope and trust play a large part as they wait, sometimes patiently, for their loved ones to come home.

An exercise in missing and remembering

Whether you and your spouse are separated by work or other commitments, the reunion is the sweet part. Do you think of that daily? One of the issues of mother's not wanting to return to the work force after giving birth is because they don't want to miss a moment of their child's development. You may wonder how much can happen in an eight-hour day, but actually a lot can happen. The baby may take their first steps during that time or say their first word. Although as adults, there won't be changes in your spouse that are significant while they are at work, but there is a part of their growing we are missing as they are living out their career with others in the same profession. They grow in relationship with their coworkers with a common understanding of their environment that in some ways are a significant part of your mate's life. You are not a part of this, or have very little invested, so these people are experiencing your spouse on another level than when you are together at home. They may see a totally different individual than you, but that's okay and very normal.

Try to remember your spouse. Take the time to sit together and talk about things that are on both of your hearts, ask how their day went, and really listen. Watch their expressions, tone, and other characteristics that are unique to them. These are memories that you want to hold onto in case of separation. Doing this exercise will also bring you awareness of how you would miss them, and what you would miss about them.

Here is an illustration of how my wife and I handle separation. When I am away at work, which is Monday through Friday in another city, we keep in contact by regular phone calls, texts, and just try to keep as close as we can. Over time, it has become normal for us to talk to each other first thing in the morning after prayers.

Then when I get to the office, I call her. She also calls me when she arrives at work at the hospital. We are very used to this pattern that sometimes I can tell when her calls will come in, and she can tell when my calls come to her. At such times, she will pick up the phone and say, "My darling is always on time."

The ultimate separation

Death can cause fear in the heart of a spouse. This separation cannot be turned around, but it's not the end either. Someone said, "That the tragedy of life is not death, but what dies inside of us while we live." To keep the hope and love alive inside of you, don't be afraid to remember those special things about your mate. They were a gift to you and enriched your marriage.

God planned for you and your spouse to be reunited once again in heaven. "Listen, I will tell you a mystery! We will not all die, but we will all be changed, in a moment, in the twinkling of an eye, at the last trumpet. For the trumpet will sound, and the dead will be raised imperishable, and we will be changed. For this perishable body must put on imperishability, and this mortal body must put on immortality" (1 Corinthians 15:51-53).[21] We have hope because of what Jesus Christ did on the cross. It is not a possibility that this will happen, it is a promise.

God knows the pain of separation. There are those who have turned their backs on God even after all he has done and would do for them. His desire is to be together with everyone for he died for the world, but because of sin, some will not join him in the joyful reunion. God will do everything he can to bring us all to him.

Although the pain of death cuts your heart, the hope of the great celebration that is coming is your hope. Leaning on this hope every day will get you to the finish line of the race God has mapped out for you. You will hear their voice again, and their laugh, but not their cries for there will be no more tears … it's a promise!

May God bless your home, and keep your marriage … in Jesus' name, Amen.

---

[21] *The Holy Bible: New Revised Standard Version,* (1 Corinthians 15:51–53), (Nashville: Thomas Nelson Publishers, 1989).

Chapter 23: Take It Easy

More marriages might survive if the partners realized that sometimes the better comes after the worse.

- Doug Larson

Our minds can create a perfect experience in our thoughts; however, when it plays out in real life, sometimes "perfect" isn't the word we would choose. Take for example people who think it is the coolest thing to go to Times Square on New Year's Eve and experience the dropping of the Waterford Crystal ball. This is what you would find out from their experience.

You would find out that it is insanely crowded on Times Square. There is no way you could drive there, and the subway would be the best mode of transportation. You must be there about 2:00 o'clock in the afternoon to be able to get any kind of a good standing place. Plus, you must not move from your spot for any reason, or you will be forfeiting your spot that you fought so hard to get. If you go with a group of people, then it might be possible for one or two to leave for a moment and have the rest of the group stand guard over your spot. So that means standing in the freezing weather for 10 hours before midnight. Dress warm.

The interesting part is that people do have a wonderful time, once they go through all the above-listed. It's a wonderful experience to gather with people for fun and celebration, remembering the past year and welcoming in the New Year. For most, it would be a once in a lifetime experience. It becomes a special memory.

Marriages can be like that, too. You have a perfect concept of what marriage will be like in your mind, but after the "I do" and "You may kiss the bride," you find that things are not perfect as first thought. That's okay. No marriage is perfect. It can't be because we are flawed humans. One thing most couples could tell you after many years of marriage is that the beginning was the roughest time. That is the time you are both learning about each other as you live under the same roof. You will see sides of your spouse that will make you think, "What have I done?" Again, this is normal.

If the differences you find with your spouse are abusive, then you need to find a safe place, but if it's not seeing things in the same way, some arguing, or feeling frustrated, that means you are both learning about each other. That is why it is written in the Bible, "If a man has recently married… for one year he is to be free to stay at home and bring happiness to the wife he has married," (Deuteronomy 24:5). God knew that adjustments needed to be made for both to become comfortable in living with each other.

Marriage at first can be like a culture shock. Nothing seems the same. One likes to eat breakfast late while the other likes it early. One's an early riser, and the other sleeps in. One likes the off-white colors, and the other likes bold colors. The list goes on and on. You will find a time when you appreciate each other's differences.

What can you do in the meantime?

Begin the day with thanking God for your spouse. List the benefits they bring to you and all the reasons you chose to marry them. Then make a commitment to give as much grace as needed to your spouse today … no matter what. You will probably need grace, too.

Pray for your spouse. If there are things that really need to be worked out and you discover there may be an ongoing problem with your spouse, come to Jesus with it. Lay your spouse in his open arms and pray for healing, grace, and mercy. God will answer. It may not be in the manner you hoped, but he is concerned and will act.

Continue to go on dates. Just because you're married that doesn't mean you stop dating. In fact, dating can help you communicate better as you are still discovering things about each other. Have fun and discover more about your spouse in a relaxed setting during your date.

Beef up your communication skills. Now is an important time to put everything you got in trying to understand each other. Don't allow Satan to get a foothold in misunderstandings. He has no place in your marriage … keep him out!

Worship and praise God together. This will not only be good for your soul, but a wonderful time of unity between you and your spouse.

Let me end this chapter with a poem:

If You Marry…

If you marry the man of your dream, life is complete.

If you marry the man of your dream, life is blissful.

If you marry the man of your dream, life is simply wonderful,

Full of love, Full of peace,

Full of sincerity, If you marry the man after your heart,

You are simply in for libidos.

If you marry the woman after your heart, life is peaceful.

If you marry the woman after your heart, life is blissful.

If you marry the woman after your heart, life is irresistible.

What is marriage without a woman after one's own heart?

It could be irksome, frustrating, neck breaking… If you marry the woman of your dream,

Life is simply the epitome of fun.

- Osaro Edosa Ogbewe

May God bless your home, and keep your marriage ... in Jesus' name, Amen.

Chapter 24: I Wanna Hold Your Hand

Show me a faithful couple and I will show you a blessed family.

– Osaro Edosa Ogbewe

Remember the first time someone from the opposite sex wanted to hold your hand? When was it? Kindergarten? No matter when it happens, it is a good feeling. Holding hands meant something special. In the elementary years, it could mean boyfriend/girlfriend or a good friend. It was kind of scary to hold hands then, as many children find ways to tease one of their peers, but they held hands anyway. Moving into middle school, holding hands is more relaxed and many of the students are doing it. High school is the same. What happens when graduation comes and perhaps marriage? The hand holding goes down. Why is that?

One of the most precious sights is seeing an elderly couple holding hands. I don't know if it's because they have lived most of their life and realize the importance of holding hands, or if they are just keeping each other from falling. It doesn't matter, for they are making a statement regarding their commitment to each other.

When was the last time you held your spouse's hand? If it has been a while, why? What message does it convey that you are nervous to share with others? Your spouse, I am sure, would love to feel the support you have for them in holding their hand. You may enjoy it yourself. Don't fear what others are going to think or say. They will probably smile at your loving gesture towards your spouse.

Supporting each other

Knowing that someone is behind you on all you do is so encouraging. Especially when it is a hard task where taking the next step can be so difficult. However, if your spouse is telling you it is the right thing to do, patting you on the back for your good work, and offering help all gives a feeling of security to a person, so that they have what is needed to go on.

Everyone needs to feel secure in their marital relationship. One way of showing that you love and care for them is by holding their hand, whispering encouragement in their ear, and helping them up when they fall. We all fall at one time or another during our life. That's part of the human experience. It's how we learn.

A pastor writes of how the support his wife shows him is valuable. "I can't imagine not having my wife's support. Pam hears what are, I'm sure, some terrible sermons in the beginning stages. But on Sunday she always has her notebook open and is eager to hear what I'm going to say. When we get home on Sunday, we can have good discussions about the sermon, because she's not somebody who's going to say, 'Boy, that was great' when it wasn't. But she's going to be there and point out what was good and helpful. That's a great source of strength to me. I guess I wouldn't be in ministry today if it weren't for her support."[22] You do not need someone to tell your everything is good, but to speak truth in a loving and supportive manner.

Acts 18 shows the loving support of missionaries Aquila and Priscilla, who were tent makers with Paul. They obviously worked together well as husband and wife in their field. Together they helped spread the gospel message and supported others like Apollos who spoke publicly by helping him see the correct truth in his message. Sometimes Priscilla's name would be listed first

---

[22] Miller, K. A. *Vol. 14: Secrets of staying power: Overcoming the discouragements of ministry,* The Leadership Library, (Carol Stream, IL; Waco, TX: Christianity Today, Inc.; Word Books 1988), 44

in the Scripture to show their equal standing. That didn't mean Priscilla dominated. It shows that Paul called her Prisca, a term of endearment but also meaning "little Priscilla."

Both Aquila and Priscilla ministered with Paul and traveled some with him, together they ministered to Apollos, and together they made tents to support their ministry. Their focus was on serving the Lord, and together they kept that focus in all they did.

In supporting one another, you are honoring God with the ministry he has given you and your spouse. You may not be a tent maker, but you may be mentoring children, helping the homeless, or showing God's love to a hurting world to draw them closer to him. In whatever you do together, show the love of Christ as you support the mate, he created just for you.

May God bless your home, and keep your marriage ... in Jesus name, Amen

Chapter 25: Become a Cuddle Bug

When I am with you, the only place I want to be is closer.

- Unknown

Being with someone you love is the best place to be. God knows that. That's why Jesus is going to meet us in heaven. The person that loves us the most will be at the gates with arms open wide to receive us. That will be one great hug!

When you are with your spouse, it feels comfortable ... and that's a good thing. You can be yourself around your spouse knowing that they love you so much. The more comfortable you feel, the more you will reveal who you really are to your spouse, and vice versa.

There are many levels of knowing another person, just like there are to knowing God. Of course, God is impossible to know completely, but as we seek him, he will allow us to see special parts of his being that will draw us closer to him. It is the same with discovering new things about your spouse. It is like a gift to receive new knowledge about who they are and how they think and feel. Getting closer is what a married couple does together. They not only cuddle on the couch, but also cuddle emotionally and cognitively, and create a safe place to reveal more of who they are and discover more of who you are. This creates a strong bond in marriage that protects the couple from divisional tactics of the enemy. The commitment the couple feels for one another become a contract where divorce is not an option. They will both do whatever else they need to do to fix the problem that could occur in their marriage.

Enjoying each other's company

What are some ways that you and your spouse can spend more time together and not get bored? It's important to find out what each of you like to do and somehow work those into your dating schedule. Even married people go on dates. If your spouse likes to go dancing, then you should be able to do that once in a while. If one loves to go to movies, that's another option. You could take turns on planning what will be done for that date. It's good to know what your spouse likes and doesn't like, so that when it's your turn to choose the activity, you can design the date night so that it will be enjoyable for your spouse, too.

It's also important to go on an adventure together … doing something neither of you have done before. Don't make it too much of a stretch like climbing Mt. Everest, but something that you may have talked about trying, but never did. There's a lot of water sports, camping, going to the theater, cooking an exotic meal, and the list goes on.

Be creative. This shared experience will be very meaningful to you and memorable. No one is the expert, and you must work together to achieve whatever you are doing. It will be a great growing time for you both.

When you can't cuddle

Being separated for a time because of work or other reason can make you want to cuddle with your spouse more than usual. It's the adage that you want what you can't have. So to get through the time without your spouse nearby, there are several things you can do to feel like you are cuddling even if it's long distance.

Write them a love email. Type in your romantic thoughts and send. Your spouse will be encouraged and feel less lonely when they receive your message.

Plan a fun activity for you two for when your spouse returns.

Make them something. Knit them a hat, bake brownies or a beautiful card.

The goal is to use your energy on something for them. This will make you feel better, and you'll be accomplishing something, too. You can celebrate their return in a fun way and read the Bible. His Spirit will touch your mind and your heart in wonderful ways. Spend some time worshiping the Lord. You will be glad you did.

Cuddle with God

When your spouse is away, this is the perfect time to have a special cuddle time with God. Let his love wrap around you as you pray as a reward for yourself that you made it through the tough time of being without them.

May God bless your home, and keep your marriage ... in Jesus' name, Amen.

Chapter 26: What's Their Opinion?

Many marriages would be better if the husband and wife clearly understood that they are on the same side.

– Zig Ziglar

Listen to good advice given before taking over a large position replacing a well-known predecessor, "Your spouse, other family members, or mature advisers may be able to bring you down from Mount Sinai for a while and give you a reality check. The first blush of enthusiasm can make you think you've been handed the chance to turn the world around for Jesus. Thank goodness for your spouse or your family, who know you're good—but not that good."[23]

Your spouse knows you well. They can be more honest with you than others, which is a good thing. You need to hear truth when it comes to big decisions.

Your spouse and you are a team. Sometimes it may not seem like it when you have differing opinions, but you must remember that both opinions are valid.

---

[23] L. Tucker, Following a Beloved Predecessor. In M. Shelley (Ed.), *Vol. 2: Empowering your church through creativity and change: 30 strategies to trans- form your ministry* (M. Shelley, Ed.) (1st ed.), Library of Christian leadership (Nashville, TN: Moorings, 1995), 278.

Always remember you are working for a common good together. The differing opinions most likely come from contrasting life experiences. Usually, there is no black or white conclusion, but a mixture of both voices on the subject will help. It is not a competition against each other, where someone is right and the other wrong.

Let's say that you and your spouse are disagreeing on what church to attend. One of you loves the big church experience. It's like having a very large family and there's always something exciting happening. The other likes a small church where everyone knows everybody and there is a feeling of closeness. So, is one right and the other wrong about the correct type of church to go to? No, both churches are valid, and the goal is to worship God. What could the solutions be?

- You could take turns going to each church and enjoy the diversity of each worship experience.

- You could each go to separate churches.

- Keep looking for a church that both would like to attend.

- There may be other suggestions also, but this will give you an idea of how to work through different opinions.

Paul's wisdom

"One person regards one day above another, another regards every day *alike*. Each person must be fully convinced in his own mind. He who observes the day, observes it for the Lord, and he who eats, does so for the Lord, for he gives thanks to God; and he who eats not, for the Lord he does not eat, and gives thanks to God. For not one of us lives for himself, and not one dies for himself; for if we live, we live for the Lord, or if we die, we die for the Lord; therefore whether we live or die, we are the Lord's" (Romans 14:5-8).[24] Paul explains here that a lot of things humans judge others on is just not worth it

---

[24] *New American Standard Bible: 1995 update*. (Romans 14:5–8), (LaHabra, CA: The Lockman Foundation, 1995).

in the long run. Unless the focus is on the Lord in all you do, your centering needs to be changed.

So when you find that you have differing opinions than your spouse, discern why there is a difference and how much it really matters in your relationship. Ask questions of your spouse regarding their opinion. Find out why they feel the way they do about the subject. This is where you will gain understanding. Then explain your feelings as clear as possible. These conversations will give each of you a deeper understanding of not only the issue, but of each other. This is a win-win situation. There are no winners and losers when opinions differ. There are only husbands and wives that are working and growing together in unity in Christ. Keep sharing your opinions with each other. You may be surprised how opinions may change for both of you.

May God bless your home, and keep your marriage ... in Jesus' name, Amen.

Chapter 27: R-E-S-P-E-C-T

Love is honesty. Love is a mutual respect for one another.

- Simone Elkeles, Leaving Paradise

When Aretha Franklin was making the song a huge hit in 1967, the Vietnam war was going along with the battle of racism. The message of respect came from the heart as a deep desire that resounded with millions of people not only then, but today. Everyone wants respect. This gives a sense of value to the person receiving the respect.

What would be some of the criteria for you to give your spouse respect? Would they need to have a nice job, be a good person, or have a lot of friends? Paul says in Ephesians 5:33, "So again I say, each man must love his wife as he loves himself, and the wife must respect her husband."[25] So basically, the respect should be mutual. Not because of anything they have done, but because they are made in the image of God.

---

[25] *Holy Bible: New Living Translation* (3rd ed.) (Ephesians 5:33), (Carol Stream, IL: Tyndale House Publishers, 2007)

Jesus's model

As Jesus is arrested, beaten and crucified, his disciples scatter. Peter is trying to follow the events of Jesus, but when someone recognizes him, he denies knowing Jesus at all. Jesus knew this would happen. The echo of the rooster crowing is painful to both Peter and Jesus.

After Jesus rises again from the dead, he appears to the disciples and other followers at different times. One time is on the beach where Peter returns to fishing with other disciples. When he sees Jesus, he is so excited he jumps out of the boat to swim to the shore. Once on shore, as he gets closer to Jesus, he hesitates—remembering his denial.

Jesus loves Peter and wants him to know that, so he shows him respect that morning. He feeds the men the fish he is cooking. Then he takes Peter aside. "When they had finished breakfast, Jesus said to Simon Peter, 'Simon son of John, do you love me more than these?' He said to him, 'Yes, Lord; you know that I love you.' Jesus said to him, 'Feed my lambs.' A second time he said to him, 'Simon son of John, do you love me?' He said to him, 'Yes, Lord; you know that I love you.' Jesus said to him, 'Tend my sheep.' He said to him the third time, 'Simon son of John, do you love me?' Peter felt hurt because he said to him the third time, 'Do you love me?' And he said to him, 'Lord, you know everything; you know that I love you.' Jesus said to him, 'Feed my sheep. Very truly, I tell you, when you were younger, you used to fasten your own belt and to go wherever you wished. But when you grow old, you will stretch out your hands, and someone else will fasten a belt around you and take you where you do not wish to go.'

(He said this to indicate the kind of death by which he would glorify God.) After this he said to him, 'Follow me.'"[26] So Jesus not only is kind to Peter, but

---

[26] *The Holy Bible: New Revised Standard Version.* (John 21:15–19), (Nashville: Thomas Nelson Publishers, 1989).

he gives him a huge responsibility in ministering to others. He also tells him about how he will die. This shows great respect in allowing Peter to know this.

Using this example in your marriage is done by showing the loving grace that Jesus offered to Peter, no matter what has happened. Again, not because of anything they have done to earn it, but because of who they are, a created being of God's. So perhaps your spouse has let you down. Jesus knows your pain. What Christ did on the cross took care of all sin … past, present, and future. If you feel you need to be compensated for evil done to you, you do not have a full understanding of God's grace. You have no right to hold anything against anyone. God commands that you forgive, even when it doesn't make sense. That's part of the mystery of Christ. It belongs to him and if there is any revenge to be taken, it is all God's and not yours. As a human, you may find that difficult to do, but I encourage you that it is not impossible. God will give you what you need to succeed, and it will greatly bless your marriage.

May God bless your home, and keep your marriage … in Jesus' name, Amen.

Chapter 28: Beat the Dog to the Door

There is no greater happiness for a man than approaching a door at the end of a day knowing someone on the other side of that door is waiting for the sound of his footsteps.

-Ronald Reagan

Who is waiting for you at home? Even if your spouse works outside of the home as well as you, you both can be anxiously awaiting seeing each other after a long day. When you think of a dog welcoming home its master, you see the epitome of excitement acted out. The dog has missed them and knows that good things happen when their person comes home. Their tail can't stop wagging.

Do you let your spouse know that you missed them while they were working and that you were praying that their day went well, and they were kept safe? This is a great thing to do, but how about welcoming them home? How can this be effectively done to where they love coming home to the welcoming arms of their spouse? It's more difficult to do when both husband and wife are working, but not impossible.

If you are at home, you have more of an opportunity to create a mood in the environment of the home when your beloved enters. You can light candles, have soft music playing, or perhaps something else they would like. Dinner could be cooking and the aroma filling the air. If you also work, there are still things you can do to create a warm and welcome home. Crock pots are great to have the meal cooking throughout the day and you both come home to a wonderful aroma. The side dishes could be prepared ahead of time, so it would only be a matter of setting them out on the table. Knowing what you both like when you get home is beneficial. Just relaxing together is very nice. Try different things and see what works for you both. Be adventurous!

Preparing mentally during the ride home

Whether your day went smooth or if it was harried, the ride home is a great opportunity to get your mind on what's important … your spouse and family. You may think your job is important, and it is, but weighing the two together, the family wins hands down. If you do not feel this way, then you need to evaluate your priorities. Anything that comes before family is not healthy. Your family is a gift given to you to enjoy, grow and protect. Get that settled in your mind before anything else.

Your work will be there the next business day when you can give of yourself again to it, but on the ride home, put work on the back burner and the family on the front … especially your spouse. Think about the possible welcome you will get by your wife and/or children. Make it the best experience for them. Plan for the possibilities of when you walk through the door. This is where memories are made, and you will be impacting their character. The joy you give to your mate and children will be a legacy passed down by generation. Pick up your children (if young enough) and hold them close telling them you love them. Ask them about their day and what interesting things they did. Use verbal and nonverbal communication that you are listening and interested.

Plan to give your spouse a big hug and kiss letting them know you truly are glad to see them. Ask them about their day. When they have finished, go ahead and share your day.

While on the ride home, play some music that you enjoy and perks up your mood. Practice smiling, even if you don't feel like it. You soon will as others smile back at you. Prepare you heart to give love to your spouse and family. Pray that they see Jesus in you.

Jesus welcomes all

The child crawled on his lap as Jesus beckoned him to come. He welcomed him and told all the people standing there that welcoming one such as he in his name is the same as welcoming Jesus. In Mark 9:36-37, this illustration speaks to how you are to welcome anyone you feel is disadvantaged in comparison to yourselves. This may or may not pertain to your spouse or children, but what about others that may be in your home when you arrive? The neighbor that needs something or just to talk, the kids next door who drive you crazy, but don't have a father or mother figure at home. Perhaps someone came in who was lonely. You must have your mind set on how you will treat them when you are home.

These acts of kindness impact the lives of your mate and children astronomically. To see Jesus with skin on transforms a person to be more like Christ. Experiencing your love and care, especially at a time you feel you would have a perfect excuse to be grouchy, honors God in huge ways. Lavish you love on your spouse and family. It's the seeds that keep on growing.

May God bless your home, and keep your marriage ... in Jesus' name, Amen.

Chapter 29: Check the Mirror

It's the little things that keep us together. Those little things will make me love you forever.

- Sonia Schaad

It's always embarrassing when you eat at a restaurant with a group, go to the restroom, look in the mirror and see evidence of your dinner stuck in your teeth for everyone to see every time you smiled, spoke, or reacted. You wished someone would have said something instead of allowing you to flash your food every time you opened your mouth. Ironically, perhaps they didn't want to embarrass you by pointing it out. Same thing with walking out of the restroom with toilet paper stuck on the bottom of your shoe, back of dress stuffed in panty hose, or forgetting to zip up. It's those little details that can derail a day for you.

It's the same thing in relating to your spouse. There may be some little things that occur that you don't really see, or don't want to see. These things stick out to others ... especially your spouse. Let's say you come home from a hard day and all you want to do is relax. You walk through the door and the kids have something to share with you from school, or your spouse wants to talk about an issue. You don't want to do anything, so you ignore them to find your solace. You probably don't realize you are doing anything wrong, but your response is like a meteor hit to those receiving it. It leaves a hole in the heart. Unless someone tells you about the impacting behavior you have, you will continue doing it every time you have a hard day. It needs to be pointed out to you so that you are aware of its danger. Talking about it is always the right thing to do. If it's not talked about, consider all the possible reasons for your response that can be conceived by your family. There are a lot of misconceived notions that can take place that don't need to by simply communicating.

How to speak the truth

The apostle Paul knew the importance of speaking truth rather than covering it up with a feel-good lie. He wrote, "...but speaking the truth in love, we are to grow up in all *aspects* into Him who is the head, *even* Christ," (Ephesians 4:15).[27] There is a purpose in speaking the truth in drawing people closer to Christ. If you simply flatter someone, they will not grow, and they may discover that you were not honest with them putting a strain on your relationship.

When you speak truth to your spouse, remember to make it as gentle as possible, still assuring them of your love and devotion, and in hopes of making your marriage even better, you bring this small concern. Obviously, this should be done when you two are alone. Don't make a big deal out of it just like you wouldn't make a big deal of parsley stuck in the teeth. These seeds of truth will make a difference in your relationship. Also, be ready to accept truth. One

truth is found in Proverbs 27:17, "Iron sharpens iron, so one man sharpens another."[28] It takes both of you in a marriage to become the best together. It is more effective to grow together than to develop by one- self. You were not meant to go through the journey of life independently. You and your spouse need each other.

---

[27] *New American Standard Bible: 1995 update,* (Ephesians 4:15), (LaHabra, CA: The Lockman Foundation, 1995).

[28] *New American Standard Bible: 1995 update.* (Proverbs 27:17), (LaHabra, CA: The Lockman Foundation. 1995).

Steps to change

When you become aware of something in your life that your spouse feels could be improved, you have a choice to make. You could either ignore their comment, procrastinate on doing anything, or take steps in improving yourself. Most likely, it will not happen overnight. For example, if your spouse told you that the amount of television that you watch is more than the time you spend with them in conversation, what would you do? You could wait until the next time it comes up thinking your spouse may have been in a bad mood at the moment. You could take steps of lessening your TV watching time and be intentional on doing something with your spouse and growing in that relationship. You may want to ask your spouse more questions about why they feel that way. The conversation will give you clarity on what they are feeling and how you can help by making a change in your routine. It's these small changes and sacrifices that make a marriage stronger and therefore successful.

May God bless your home, and keep your marriage ... in Jesus' name, Amen.

Chapter 30: Flirting

I love it when I catch you looking at me then you smile and look away.

- Unknown

Do you remember the first time you looked into each other's eyes? It may have felt uncomfortable, but you kept staring anyway. You were locked in. Then like some magical moment of wake-up, one of you looks away shyly. Then maybe looks again. This is a sample of flirting. You can tell because only two people are involved, you are drawn in and your toes curl up. Okay, maybe not the last part, but it may feel like it.

When you and your spouse have been married for years, sometimes the flirtation stops. You may think you no longer have to draw a person's interest to win them over. As a married person, we should still woo our partner to keep the romance alive. Remember how fun it was to flirt? Even if you are married it is still fun. You may not remember how to flirt, so let me give you a few tips.

- Flirting is unexpected. Choose a time when it would be not normal behavior from you. This makes it spontaneous, which always adds to the mystery of you. Mystery is good.

- Flirt only with your spouse. Do not practice on others. This could be highly dangerous to your relationship (and your health).

- Make sure the flirting you do to your spouse is not derogatory. You want them to feel special, not dirty. The message you want them to receive is that I love you and think you are the most beautiful/handsome person in the world, and I'm so glad you're mine.

- Flirting is a combination of both verbal and physical communication. It could be the way you look at them or touch their arm. Many times, unspoken communication is more powerful than words.

- If they smile, you are doing it right.

I flirt with my wife all the time, and she enjoys it. One incident, I deliberately opened the bathroom door knowing she was having her bath.

"What are you looking for?" she screamed lovingly.

"My shoe!" I replied. We both burst out laughing uncontrollably. What would a shoe be doing inside the bathroom you may ask? Well, it is all part of flirting, and it was fun.

It is also worthy to note that not all women or men understand this language and may find it rather offensive or embarrassing. Well, caution is the rule. You should be able to know your mate enough to know what angers them or makes them smile. I urge you to go ahead and flirt with your mate. You may be so amazed at the positive outcome.

Physical flirting

One way to physically flirt is to kiss the neck and shoulders of your spouse. They could be doing dishes or cooking a meal. This is a fun and meaningful action for it makes them feel loved by you.

You may know of another spot on your spouse's body where if you touch it, it brings a response, for example, licking their earlobe, tracing their body with your finger, or tracing the lines in the palm of their hand and fingers. The hands are very sensitive to touch.

Physical touch is a very effective flirtation tool you can use to express your ongoing desire for your spouse. Where is your spouse now? Is it time for a little flirting practice? I can see you smile...

When not to flirt

If you can see that your spouse is upset or worried about something, this probably is not a good time to flirt. It may be understood as you not taking their feelings into consideration at the moment. You want to be sensitive to their needs.

It is important to note that it may not be appreciated if you flirt with your spouse in front of others. It may be embarrassing to them or bring unwanted attention. You may have heard the saying, "Get a room." That means others don't want to watch as you show affection to each other. Keep your flirtation antics to where only the two of you enjoy it. This is very important.

Flirting is an art

Any art needs to be practiced, so keep up with the flirting towards your spouse, and you can become a master at it. Consider the great flirts who have gone before you: Groucho Marx, Gomez Addams (The Addams Family), Jack Sparrow and more. However, you could also read the Song of Solomon in the Bible and see how he flirts with his beloved.

May God bless your home, and keep your marriage ... in Jesus' name, Amen.

Chapter 31: Celebrate Their Life

Family: Where life begins and love never ends.

-Unknown

Isn't it fun to celebrate? You have so many opportunities to do this with your beloved. There are birthdays, anniversaries, new job, new house, good grades, and a myriad of other events. Celebration brings people closer together and it will bring you and your spouse closer, too.

Celebrate your spouse

Your spouse is a gift to you every day. If you look for a reason to celebrate your spouse daily, you will find it. It isn't difficult to do. Celebrations come in all sizes from large to small. Even if you celebrate your spouse in some small way, it will make a difference in your relationship. Can you imagine what it would feel like to be celebrated every day?

Celebration is an expression of being thankful. It isn't what you have in your pocket that makes you thankful, but what you have in your heart. Think of the many ways you are thankful for your spouse. These are indicators of celebration. If you love how your spouse makes lasagna, that doesn't mean you have to get balloons and candy (unless you want to), but it means to have an attitude of celebration. Show your joy in being able to eat their lasagna that day. If you love how they can easily fix the car when it is broken, celebrate that. Show your joy in driving the car with them. Maybe take them for a special date in the car. These are the smaller celebrations, but still important.

The bigger celebrations may take a bit more effort on your part, but it will be worth it. The special events in your spouse's life mean a lot to them, and they want to think that it means a lot to you, too. So prove to them that it does by being intentional on celebration.

The benefits of celebration

There are many benefits to celebrating. Life can seem difficult and the burdens heavy that many carry. These can be lightened by focusing on the good things in life, being thankful, and expressing it by celebration. It really makes you and your spouse feel good to think about the successes you have in life. You have been there for each other to love and support as goals or targets were met. This will encourage continual engagement of each other's needs to meet goals and targets.

Positive thinking can result from celebrating. Knowing the good you and your spouse have accomplished sets a model for success. The certainty that "you can do this" makes a person stronger inside and more confident. The fear of trying something else will not be as apparent as before. You will be ready to go on to the next adventure.

There are many health benefits to celebrating because it is fun. Fun brings your blood pressure down and extends your life. Isn't that enough reason to celebrate? How about the "feel good" endorphins that are released. They are priceless. When you feel good, you can think clearer and have more of a positive spin on your life. The negative thoughts fade into the background. A stressful life is a dying life!

So you can see that celebrating is a very good thing to do. Celebrating your spouse will have other benefits in the romantic realm. Your spouse will respond to the kindness you show them through expressing your happiness to having them in your life. It is so touching to the soul.

Steps of Celebrating

As you think about how or what to celebrate for your spouse, consider the following ideas to determine the next expression of gratefulness:

- Review the last 24 hours of what your spouse has done for you. List everything you can think of—big or small.

- What impact did each item on the list have on you?

- Would it have made a difference if they didn't do it?

- Brainstorm how you can celebrate (keep these ideas for future use)

- Enjoy!

God loves a thankful heart. As you celebrate, you are thanking him for the gift of your spouse. It is a style of worship that he honors and will join in with his Holy Spirit. Let's celebrate!

May God bless your home, and keep your marriage ... in Jesus' name, Amen.

Chapter 32: Say You're Sorry

The first to apologize is the bravest. The first to forgive is the strongest. The first to forget is the happiest.

– Unknown

Allison was looking forward to spending time with her husband— even if it was at a car show. Robert had been so busy at work that they seemed more distant in their relationship. They lived in the same house and saw each other occasionally as they passed to go in their separate directions. She wanted more.

Bling!

She looked at the text she just received. "*Sorry, honey, need to cancel. Business problem.*" Robert was canceling; she couldn't believe it. The business problem was obviously more important than the relationship problem, she thought. Tears spilled from her eyes as she sat wondering what to do.

"Honey. Wake up," Robert nudged gently.

Allison realized she must have fallen asleep. "Hi, I guess I fell asleep. What time is it?"

"It's time to go to the car show. As soon as I sent that text to you, my spirit cringed and I knew I needed to come home and spend time with you. I am so sorry for neglecting you. Please forgive me."

She answered with a kiss.

******

It's a part of human nature to hurt someone—even the ones you love. It's not intentional most of the time, but it does occur. So what do you do to counteract the hurt you caused? Perhaps you were taught as a small child to say, "I'm sorry." You did it then probably because you were made to, but did the lesson stick of why you said you were sorry?

Apologizing brings healing to a hurtful situation. You have the power to express sorrow for an action you did, or may have been involved in. Peace needs to be restored and you can initiate this for the other person by saying you're sorry. Saying you are sorry is not a sign of weakness or defeat.

Apologizing to your spouse is important for they are with you through thick and thin. You are committed to them to share life together. If they hurt, you hurt. If you find this is not true for you, then you may have to deal with another issue called self. If you are not emotionally connected with your spouse, you need to take steps to draw closer.

The gift to your spouse

There may be a time when something you have said and/or done has hurt your spouse. Even though you may have been correct in what you said or did, is it worth being right to see the pain in your spouse's eyes? What if you apologized anyway? Wouldn't that gift be worth seeing their smile light up the room again? You may think, but it wouldn't be true. Remember what Jesus said regarding love covers a multitude of sin. God's love covers it. Your love covers it. Love is the strong foundation that you and your spouse stand on. Plus, you may think you are right, but you may not see the scope of all things. Perceptions play a lot into our decisions, and they are not always correct.

Consider the grace that you have been shown throughout life, and include the all-encompassing grace of Jesus, and that should be more than enough to be

144

able to say I'm sorry to your spouse with full love and grace in your heart. Give the gift they can keep on giving. You will be setting a model for others.

How to say you're sorry

You are going to apologize to your spouse, but you're unsure of how to do it correctly. Here are a few tips to help you:

- Make sure you fully understand the offense. You cannot effectively apologize without knowing this. Remember, this is not a time to get your spouse to agree with you, you are simply giving them a gift of grace.

- Ask for a moment alone with your spouse. If family is around, you may have to go to another room or outside.

- Look them directly in the eye and tell them your understanding of the offense and that you want to apologize.

- Tell them you're sorry and why.

- Assure them that they mean more to you than this. You hate to see them in pain of any kind.

- Ask for their forgiveness.

Saying I'm sorry should become a natural occurrence when needed. The peace you give to your spouse and to yourself is well worth the effort.

May God bless your home, and keep your marriage ... in Jesus' name, Amen.

Chapter 33: Forgiveness is the Key

A happy marriage is the union of two good forgivers.

- Ruth Bell Graham

It had been a month since the incident. Sarah's heart ached as she thought about it. Branden cheated on her, and she can't bring herself to move forward from it. Each day felt like she was carrying sandbags over her shoulders. Doing anything took a lot of effort.

Branden walked into the room. "I'm going to the park. Would you like to walk with me?"

"I don't know."

"Sarah, I am so sorry how I've hurt you. It was so stupid of me. I'm going to counseling, have accountability partners, and repented to God. Can't you please find it in your heart to forgive me?"

"I really want to, Branden. Emotionally, I don't feel like I can yet, but I know I need to. I don't want to live the rest of my life like this."

******

Forgiveness is a gift given to someone who doesn't deserve it. Who would that be? Look in the mirror. God has forgiven us not on our merit, but on the grace of Jesus.

Like Brendan and Sarah, many married couples must deal with forgiving one another. If emotions were the key to forgiveness, none of us would make it for very long. The key to forgiveness is Jesus. Trusting God with the offense rather than yourself makes a difference.

Why should you forgive your spouse? There are many benefits, but the main reason you are to forgive is because God said so. The offenses made against you may be small or large, but the result is the same regarding forgiveness. This does not mean to turn a blind eye to the sin, but to forgive and allow God to work. It's difficult to trust the Lord to turn the ashes into beauty, but he can do it. We cannot "forgive and forget" for we are human and remember the hurts against us. However, in forgiving, we become free from allowing the hurts to control us. We are set free to move on. So giving the gift of forgiveness benefits you both.

What forgiveness is not

To help you clarify what forgiveness is, it is first important to say what it is not. You may have confusing feelings about forgiveness because you may have some wrong ideas about it. It conflicts in your mind and that is where the difficulty of being able to forgive exists.

Forgiveness is not saying that what happened to you is okay. It's not okay. You were hurt. To say it was okay is like saying that you don't matter. That is not true. What God would like you to do is turn it all over to him and trust that he will take care of it perfectly. Put the heaviness on God's shoulders. He can take it. "Casting all your care upon him; for he careth for you" (1 Peter 5: 7 KJV).

Forgiveness is not saying the person who offended you was right, and you were wrong. It has nothing to do with right and wrong. It has everything to do with releasing yourself from the prison of not forgiving.

As mentioned before, forgiveness is not forgetting. We humanly can't forget, but we can move on because it no longer controls us.

Benefits of forgiving

Forgiveness brings freedom for both you and your spouse. You do not need to be controlled by the hurt any more. You are free to move on and allow the hurt to heal.

You and your spouse will become closer as healing occurs. Healing may come quicker with the help of a counselor to direct you both if the offense is difficult. The commitment made by you two to forgive will build a strong foundation in your relationship.

You will be given peace of mind in forgiving. It's the peace of Jesus that passes understanding. It's the peace that you can live and have others see and experience it and giving God the glory.

Forgiveness affects the mind, body, and soul. God wants you to be well, do you?

Loosening your grip

If you are holding on to the offense and not allowing forgiveness to occur, you may have a control issue. You may believe that in not forgiving someone for an offense keeps you in control of it. It is not true. It only keeps you imprisoned. You must release it to become free.

In loosening your grip on the offense and forgiving your spouse, you are in a sense tightening your grip on God's hand. That's a good thing. Don't let go. His hand will take you and your spouse to a higher level in your relationship—more than you can imagine.

May God bless your home, and keep your marriage ... in Jesus' name, Amen.

Chapter 34: Romantic Encounters

Romance is the glamour which turns the dust of everyday life into a golden haze.

- Elinor Glyn

His hand touches hers. Evie stops breathing for a moment. She thinks today would be routine in serving the customers at the Big Star Restaurant. But William J., her cowboy, changes all that when he walks in. They had been married for close to twenty years now, but when he touches her, it is like lightening coursing through her being.

******

Your spouse is your romantic interest. How do you "fire up" that interest between the two of you? Is it a look or a word? Perhaps it's a touch like Evie's story. Whatever mode you choose, you know the importance of keeping romance in the relationship ... right? After being married a few years, you may have forgotten that as many others have done. You may even be thinking right now, how do I do that?

Start dating: Remember the fun you had going on dates with your spouse. No cares in the world just spending time together and learning more about each other. You would laugh together and enjoy each other's company. There would be mystery between you two. You didn't know fully how the other felt about you, so you were always on your best behavior. A lot of attention went into how you looked. You had so much to learn about each other back then.

You still have things to learn about each other. It is just at a different level now. You can go deeper to find out what they are thinking and feeling. Dating allows you both to focus only on you two. Make yourself look good. That shows how important your spouse is to you. You can have fun together, go out dancing, play a sport, visit the zoo, etc. The list is infinite of the many things you can do together to recapture the romance you once had. It's there. It just needs a little kindling to get it fired up again. You never know how well romance can get again until you try. Don't see yourself as too old for this.

Go to bed at the same time: Perhaps you both have different sleeping habits, but try to go to bed together and enjoy the time of snuggling. You and your spouse may have a great discussion before nodding off. Sleeping together at the same time will bring you closer.

Get fun sleepwear: The flannels can go back in the drawer. Find something for you to wear that your spouse may find sexy. Silky and lacy are considered very romantic.

Keep it fresh: Routine is boring. Leave a little mystery about yourself with your spouse. Keeping them intrigued keeps them interested. Do something different.

Leave love notes: It's special to anyone to receive love notes. To have feelings and thoughts written out touches the heart of your spouse. It doesn't need to be a formal poem, although that would be great if you have that talent. It only needs to be a few words of love from you. It will be so appreciated.

Return to the courtesies: When you first dated, you probably opened the door for your spouse, watched what words you used, offered them the bigger piece of dessert and so on. Doing it again will rekindle the memories of dating. Treating each other special like this every day in marriage is touching.

Go on a bike ride/hiking for the afternoon: The adventure of being outside and biking or walking towards a goal gives a spirit of adventure. Find a beautiful spot where the two of you can spend some time together. Maybe take a picnic lunch along.

Make a special dinner for your spouse: You probably know their favorite foods, so put together a feast for just the two of you. Light candles, put soft music on, have wine chilling, and if you have children, perhaps a night at the grandparents for them.

Massage oil: Nothing feels better than having a massage with oil that smells divine. Warm the oil in your hands and begin rubbing the tired muscles of your spouse. They will never forget this moment.

******

As you can see, there are many ways to bring romance into the forefront of your marriage. Hopefully, the suggestions above will get your creative juices moving. Your relationship started on a romantic basis, and there's no reason not to have the romance back and ongoing. It may feel unnatural at first but give it time. Soon it will become a romantic habit every day. Fall in love with your spouse all over again.

May God bless your home, and keep your marriage ... in Jesus' name, Amen.

Chapter 35: Ask Caring Questions

In marriage, each partner is to be an encourager rather than a critic, a forgiver rather than a collector of hurts, an enabler rather than a reformer.

-H. Norman Wright and Gary Oliver

"There's no lunch meat for my sandwich again. Wasn't it on the grocery list?" Derek slammed the refrigerator door.

"Honey, I'm sorry. I didn't get a chance to get to the store today. Let me make you some egg salad." Rachel got up from the table and walked towards the stove.

"Forget it ... I gotta go. See you tonight." He walked out the door without even a glance.

When Derek got to work, his boss was at his desk.

"Where is the Robert's report? Wasn't that supposed to be on my desk this morning?" his boss said.

"I'm sorry, sir. I've been so busy with the Thompson project; I haven't had time to get to it yet. Let me do it right now for you." As Derek reached for it, his boss snatched it back.

"Never mind, I'll do it myself," he said walking back into his office and slamming the door.

Derek felt worthless. He looked at the picture of Rachel on his desk and realized he had done the same thing to her back home.

******

Humans have the capability to be so loving, but also be so callous in their treatment of each other. Unfortunately, we all have the callous gene that makes us say and do things we wished we hadn't. We have hurt the people closest to us with our careless words and deeds because we are mainly thinking of ourselves rather than the other person.

You however have an opportunity to do this better. Your spouse needs to be cared for and listened to by you. Ask caring questions to hear more about what is going on with them. Let the focus be on their cares rather than yours. Be mindful of the things they needed to do that day and ask how they went. Your attention to them in remembering what they were doing that day and asking about it will greatly impress your spouse and put happiness into your marriage.

Use encouraging words

It really doesn't take much to tear someone down with words, but it takes a lot more work for someone to be built up again. The tools to use in this kind of rebuilding project are encouraging words. You can help your spouse face anything more confidently by a word of encouragement from you. Your spouse loves you and respects your opinion of what they can and can't do. So telling them they can will help them do it. Building their confidence by what you say to them will bring your relationship closer, because they love the support from you. They have worth.

The art of asking good caring questions

A good caring question will help your spouse think about their answer and reflect on it before verbalizing it. The question will show that the one asking it, you, really cares about them. It is not a question to make them feel uncomfortable, but to encourage them. They feel secure in answering it and have no fear of being judged.

Here are a few examples of good caring questions:

- What gave you the most joy today and why?

- What do you think will be the greatest part of your day tomorrow? Why?

- How can I help you live your dreams?

These questions are filled with hope and encouragement. Care and concern is voiced along with support. Your spouse will feel cherished by your expression of love. As they thoughtfully answer these questions, ask follow-up questions for clarity and showing you are truly interested in what they have to say.

Invite your spouse to ask questions

Perhaps your spouse has wondered something about you for quite a while but hasn't asked you for whatever reason. Give them an opportunity to ask. Simply say, "Is there anything you wanted to ask me about? I would be happy to answer your questions." You want this to remain a safe environment for your spouse, so if they ask a question you don't want to answer, just tell them you don't feel ready to talk about that right now but will let them know when you are ready.

Questions are at the heart of learning. Jesus used them often with his disciples to help them grasp the reality of the kingdom. Keep seeking and learning about your spouse by asking caring questions. You will grow closer each day as you share.

May God bless your home, and keep your marriage ... in Jesus' name, Amen.

Chapter 36: The Power of Being Positive

Happily ever after is not a fairy tale. It's a choice.

- Fawn Weaver

"We are never going to get out of debt," John said as he went through the monthly bills. "How are we going to get the maintenance done on this house? It's falling apart around us?"

Julie tried to remain calm and cool. "Yes, I know things are tight right now, but they will get better."

"How are they going to get better?"

"Well, we are saving money here and there and that is adding up.

We will get ahead soon. God knows our needs."

John was obviously not convinced. His body wore the stress of providing for his family.

"The best thing though," Julie continued, "... is that we have each other. That makes me the happiest."

He looked at her and smiled. "Me, too. I suppose you're right.

Things will get better."

******

Helping your spouse see the positive side of a situation helps them to move on in a better spirit than to focus on what's wrong. This is a gift you can give to your spouse. This does not mean to be blind to situations that need attention, but to not put their entire time and energy thinking about it. When that happens, there is so much life missed.

God has so many wonderful things for us each day that he doesn't want us to miss. They are gifts from him to us, his children. We need to be aware of them to receive them and be grateful.

How to help your spouse be positive

Sometimes this can be quite the challenge if your spouse naturally leans toward the negative, but it is possible. Here are a few ideas of how you can help your mate be positive:

- Count your blessings: This is an old idea, but a good one. Help your spouse consider all the wonderful things God has done for them. Also, share with them the good things of your day.

- Make a plan: If a situation is really bothering your spouse, make a plan together to fix it. This may take some time to get it resolved, but sometimes seeing it in a workable plan helps them see it is being taken care of, but it will just take a little time.

- Spoil them: Make them a favorite meal, get their slippers and newspaper for them, give them a back rub, or anything else that would make them feel good about being home.

- Smile: There is power in a smile. When you smile at your spouse, it will be difficult for them not to return the smile.

- Give them a time to be negative: If they are feeling negative, allow them to get it out of their system for an allotted amount of time. Tell them to get it out, and then go for ice cream.

- Help them see the beauty of creation: Go out for a walk with your spouse or take them to the beach or some other pretty setting and enjoy it together.

As you can see, there are many ways you can turn their negativity into a positive outlook. Of course, they must choose to do that. Sometimes they just don't want to, and you must respect that choice. If it seems like they are getting depressed, you may want to suggest that perhaps talking about it to a counsellor would help. You don't want to leave your beloved in a negative state for a long period of time.

Perhaps you are the one struggling to be positive. You have learned how to be negative since day one and you aren't about to let it go. As a gift to your spouse, let it go. Show them a positive side to you. They will be quick to notice it and be drawn to it. This is a choice you need to make. Your outlook can be good or bleak. Your attitude affects others, so if you want a spouse who is negative, then keep doing the same, but if you want a refreshment of the spirit, you need to make a commitment to change your mind and be transformed. You would be surprised how much it would change your relationship with your spouse.

Read God's promises

There is nothing more positive than the promises of God. Read them together as a couple every day and drink in the truth of how good he is to you both. Believe what he says and live it. Praise God from whom all blessings flow.

May God bless your home, and keep your marriage ... in Jesus' name, Amen.

Chapter 37: Kindness Wins!

A good marriage is a contest of generosity.

- Diane Sawyer

Abby was tired. She slumped down the stairs with her robe on and headed for the kitchen. Walking in she noticed that the kitchen was totally cleaned. Coffee was made ... and smelled so good. As she went to the cupboard to get a cup, her husband, Alan, walked in from outside.

"Good morning, sleepyhead. I was just out cleaning your car."

Abby looked at him with an unsure look on her face. "Okay, what's going on? The kitchen is clean, coffee made, and now you cleaned my car. Is it my birthday?"

He kissed her on the cheek. "No, honey. I just want to show you how much I love you. I know I haven't done it a lot in the past, but I want to try now to make up for it."

She set her coffee on the table. "I see ..." Abby walked over to a lower cupboard and pulled out a frying pan. She then went to the refrigerator and took out the egg carton and bacon.

"So, what are you doing?" he asked.

"I'm making you eggs and bacon for breakfast. Two can play this game." She smiled at him.

"Oh, this is going to be fun," Alan said excitedly as he sat at the table waiting for breakfast.

******

Sometimes it's easier to be kind to a stranger than it is to someone close to you. You want to give the impression of kindness to someone that doesn't know you very well, and your intentions may be pure in truly wanting to be kind, but somehow it gets lost when you come home. You don't feel the pressure to be kind there. The family loves you any way; however, your show of kindness is needed more at home.

Think about the transformation that could happen in your relationship with your spouse if you focused on being kind to them. They will really wonder what's up. You will add some mystery to the relationship. It will truly feel good to you to see your spouse smile because of a kind thing you did for them. The atmosphere in your home will change to one more positive. There are countless benefits to being kind to your spouse. Start today in making their day.

Ideas of kindness

To get you started, here are some ideas on kindness. The list is endless, and you will think of more ways of kindness, but in case you're not sure what to do, these will give you an inkling.

- Clean the bathroom. That's right, if your spouse is the one who always cleans it or another spot in the house, take a turn.
- Help them carry heavy things.
- Bring them breakfast in bed.
- Take them out for coffee or tea.
- Give them a gift card to their favorite place to go.
- Allow them to watch their favorite shows on television.
- If they are leaving on business, help them pack. Maybe add a little note

164

or other surprise for them in their suitcase.

- Before going to bed, turn down the bed on their side and put a mint on the pillow.
- Shine their shoes.
- Open doors for them.
- Say please and thank you.
- Tell them what a great job they did on something.

To be kind is to be encouraging and empowering to your spouse. You are giving them "prince" or "princess" moments that show that they have great value to you. Their priceless value to you comes from sharing life together, experiencing adventures that only you both had. You have grown to love them more and more each day and can't imagine life without them. They are definitely worth being kind to in your eyes.

Consider the kindness that God shows you every day. He has blessed you abundantly with kindness. The kindness God blesses you with is so that you can bless others. Who better to bless than the one you have devoted your life to and committed to love every day of your life so long as you both shall live.

May God bless your home, and keep your marriage ... in Jesus' name, Amen.

Chapter 38: Tending the Garden

Marriages, like a garden, take time to grow. But the harvest is rich unto those who patiently and tenderly care for the ground.

- Darlene Schacht

The young boy watched as his grandfather weeded the garden. There were vegetables on one side and beautiful flowers on the other.

"Grandpa, why do you work so hard every day in the garden picking out each weed? The plants would be okay if a couple were left there, wouldn't they?"

"Well, Eric, if I left a few of the weeds in, they may take some of the nutrients I want for the vegetables and flowers. They would become weak and fail. Weeds multiply fast, so I must make sure I get them all. Your grandma wants her flowers to be beautiful, too."

"You and grandma have been married a long time. Seems like a lot of my friends' parents are getting divorced."

"Marriage is like a garden. It needs to be tended every day so that all the weeds of the world don't drain it. Your grandma and I have been weeding our marriage for years. The garden of love we have grown gives us joy."

******

If you have had a garden, you know how important it is to work on it often. Weeds can overtake the plants, it can become dry if you don't water it and it doesn't rain, and animals can eat your crop if you don't put protective elements around it. There is a lot that needs to be done with a garden. There's finding a good sunny spot for it, tilling the soil, planting the seeds, watering it, and weeding it. These are all parts of enjoying a healthy garden.

A marriage is also like a garden in that it needs to be based in a good "sunny" spot ... like under God's love. If a marriage isn't based on Christ, it is likely to allow the weeds of the world in that will strangle the love and kill the marriage. Planting a home on fertile soil of growth and happiness will give a couple the best chances for success.

Tilling the soil of a marriage is getting all the rocks and weeds out before planting good seeds. The good seeds of God's love can take root in a marriage free of debris from the world. The debris are those things that are not of God, like materialism, self, addictions, and the list is endless. These things can wreak havoc in a marriage and can drain its energy leaving a very weak couple that longs to keep it together but is unable to do so.

Planting the seeds of God into your marriage is done through the daily reading of his Word and prayer. These seeds will take root in the hearts of both you and your spouse.

Watering the seeds with the living water of Jesus will keep them fresh and

bearing much fruit. Living out the fruit of the Spirit in your marriage will give it strength to withstand the most difficult challenges that can happen. Give your spouse love, joy, peace, forbearance, kindness, goodness, faithfulness, gentleness, and self- control. These nutrients will strengthen the marriage and keep it strong and happy.

The weeding process comes when things come into the marriage that don't belong there like abuse, self-focus, addictions, pride, arrogance, sexual impurity, and general bad choices of temptations that have led them to darkness. God gets His gardening tools out and starts picking away at the weeds and rocks to get them out. However, it is your choice to take the weed out of your life. Being free from these weeds will give a good growing soil to your marriage.

So what does your garden look like? Is your marriage full of weeds that need to be extracted, or maybe refreshed with God's living water? Take some time to tend your garden. Look at the different ways you can make it better. You need to spend time with God. That is the most important thing. But right after it is spending time with your spouse. This is good quality time that will enrich your hearts and make your marriage stronger. Pray together. There is power in prayer, and it will empower your marriage.

May God bless your home, and keep your marriage ... in Jesus' name, Amen.

Chapter 39: Communicate Your Love

Love is a promise; love is a souvenir, once given never forgotten, never let it disappear.

– John Lennon

As Shelly was opening her lunch bag, she noticed something tucked inside. A small envelope with her name on it. She opened it and read, *My darling, I just wanted you to know that you are in my thoughts and prayers today. I love you and hope you are experiencing God's best for you. Love, Dan*

Shelly knew she just experienced the best part of her day. *Thank you, God!*

******

Expressing love can be a difficult thing to do, but only because of your fears. Some of the fears that get in your way are rejection, saying the wrong thing, hurting the other person, looking like a fool, and a myriad of other things that don't really have any weight except for what you give it. You allow these fears to take you away from a higher level of love to experience with your spouse. That doesn't need to happen any longer.

The choice that you will make today is to express your love to your spouse every opportunity that you get. Nothing will hold you back. You want the fulness of your love to be known to your spouse. No longer will your passion be passive. You have a lifetime of love to give to your beloved and it's a great investment to make. Your love for each other will multiply and grow to abundance.

Communication methods

As you probably know, there are many ways that you can communicate love to your spouse. Consider using the five senses: sight, audio, touch, taste, and smell. These senses are given to you to bring more enjoyment to your life experience, along with giving you more information to fully understand communication from others or your environment.

Sight: There used to be a song that stated, "The look of love is in your eyes." Can your spouse see that look in you? Are your eyes trained on them in those moments of love? It's a look that expresses the deep passion you have for them.

Other ways for your spouse to see your love is by doing things for them such as helping with the cleaning, home projects, or in other areas. Bringing them a gift such as flowers is a constant reminder of your love each time they see the gift. Love notes are wonderful for the eyes and heart, too.

Audio: How does your spouse hear your love? The most obvious is hearing the words, "I love you." However, there are other ways a spouse can hear your love for them. Could you write a poem or song and perform it to them? It doesn't need to be perfect ... just heartfelt.

You could say encouraging words to them throughout the day. Compliment them on how they look and what they do. If they are feeling down, lift them up with encouraging words. Another way to lift their spirits and to show your love is to play a song that is meaningful to them. Music can bring them back to a very special time in their lives. They will truly appreciate your thoughtfulness.

Touch: One of the most expressive ways to communicate your love is by touch. This is not limited to sex, although that is definitely a part of it. Touching your spouse in a manner that is only meant for them tells them they are special to you. Make sure that all your touching not only communicates your love for them, but your respect. Touching that only fulfills your sexual desire is selfish.

Giving hugs, kisses, holding hands, putting an arm around their waist or shoulders, nuzzling, and more communicates your love to be with them. Giving massages with oil is a wonderful and fun way to communicate your love for your spouse. Giving pleasure through touch sends an amazing message of love.

Taste: An exquisite dinner just for you two speaks love. Chocolate or another favorite treat that you surprise them with shows your thoughtfulness. You want to give them something that gives great pleasure to their palate. This communicates love.

Taste can create great memories. Many remember Grandma's cooking and the love she put into her cookies. That is a love memory created by taste. This type of memory can be created by you for your spouse. Enjoy the flavors of love.

Smell: A rose is a rose is a rose. What makes the rose such a symbol of love? It is beautiful, but it is the fragrant aroma that surrounds it that makes it so enticing. Like taste, smell also has a strong memory that runs throughout an individual's life.

Creating these memories for your spouse will allow them to remember your love for them every time they smell the reminder.

Think of fresh baked bread, a turkey on Thanksgiving, or the bouquet of a fine wine. These are powerful enough memories to begin drooling. These kinds of aromas take a person back to when the memory was made and helps them relive it just a bit. You can create these memories for your spouse by brewing a favorite flavor of coffee, lighting a scented candle, or giving them a massage using scented oil. The memories you created together will last forever.

Communicating love is not difficult, but it must be done. It is an investment in the special relationship between you two and well worth the time and effort. Communicate your love to your spouse today.

May God bless your home, and keep your marriage ... in Jesus' name, Amen.

Chapter 40: Reminiscing

"Marriage. It's like a cultural handrail. It links folks to the past and guides them to the future."

-Diane Frolov

Looking through the photographs, Zoe felt tears run down her cheeks. It has been 10 years since her husband, Greg, died in action in Iraq. He was on a special mission that went terribly wrong. She misses him every day and wishes that she could have been pregnant before he left, so that she could have a little piece of him with her to hold and love. But it is not to be.

Closing their wedding album, she put it back in the cabinet. To reminisce on the day of her husband's death is painful. She can't focus and doesn't know what to do with herself.

Buzz!

She walks to the intercom by her door and pushes the button. "Hello."

"Hi Zoe. It's Mark. I just thought I would stop by and see how you are doing today."

Mark was Greg's brother. He had been so helpful to her through the years after Greg's death. She pushes the button to unlock the front door of the apartment building. Within a couple minutes, there is a tap on the door. She opens it to find Mark standing there with flowers for her.

"Just want to brighten your day," he said handing them to her.

"That is so thoughtful. Thank you, Mark. Come in and have a seat. I was just crying over the wedding album."

"Ah, that answers why you have streaky eyes." He smiles at her and pats her hand. Big tough guys get away with crying ... no makeup.

Zoe laughs. "You are brightening my day. Thank you."

"How would you like to go out and celebrate Greg's life by doing something he always loved to do ... going out for ice cream."

"He did have a sweet tooth for that ... butter pecan."

"His favorite," Mark said.

"Well, I'm game. It's better than sitting here depressed."

"Greg wouldn't want that ... he always loved your laugh."

"Thanks for reminding me."

******

Reminiscing is a wonderful way to remember the good times in life. The happy memories delight you and your spouse's hearts. Reliving these moments bring the two of you closer in your relationship realizing the many experiences you shared.

Of course, there is the other side of remembering the sad and difficult times together. It is also important to reflect on these parts of the journey because that is where most of the growth and strength was experienced by you two. The lessons learned are invaluable. The tears shed ... priceless. It is through these experiences that you saw the love your spouse has for you and where you could express your love for them. It is unconditional. You carried each other through with your love.

Memories are the most precious things we have because they are only for us. They are something that cannot be taken away from us. Each time we relive them, it warms our heart and shows us how fragile life is and how good it can be.

So how can you help your spouse reminisce and experience their best loved life events all over again? Can you imagine how romantic it would be to reenact your first date? That would be so heartfelt and lovely for your spouse. Perhaps you can go back to the place where you became engaged. Celebrating the important moments of your relationship is a form of reminiscing.

You can verbally reminisce with your spouse by sharing your thoughts when you first laid eyes on them. How did they look to you? Were you afraid to talk to them or ask them out? What was it that drew you to them? Sharing what you experienced inside will give your spouse insight to how special they are to you.

God gives you these moments to enjoy. Reminiscing shows your gratefulness to God for these moments. It allows you and your spouse to once again be overjoyed by his gift and to praise him for it.

May God bless your home, and keep your marriage ... in Jesus' name, Amen.

Chapter 41: Who's Your BFF?

In marriage, each partner is to be an encourager rather than a critic, a forgiver rather than a collector of hurts, an enabler rather than a reformer.

- H. Norman Wright and Gary Oliver

Carly and Jess sat in the booth enjoying their nachos. It was a calming atmosphere with the Spanish guitar playing softly. They hadn't seen each other in nearly a year.

"So Jess, what have you been up to lately? You said you were dating someone special."

"Yes, his name is Darren. We've been seeing each other for about six months. I really like being with him."

"That is an indication of a good relationship knowing that you like being with each other. I know that's how I feel about James. He is my BFF."

"BFF? Your husband?" Jess asked.

"Yes, I consider James my best friend forever. We have enjoyed being together from the beginning. I can share my secrets with him knowing that he locks them deep inside himself. I love him, but I re- ally like him, too."

"Thank you for sharing that. My goal is also to have my future husband be my BFF. It is possible. You are living proof of that."

******

Someone once said, "The best antique is an old friend." What makes a good friend? They are people you like to hang around with, go places, and do things together. They can make you laugh and bring you to tears. Your deepest secrets are safe with them, and you never fear them hurting you intentionally. You can be yourself feeling totally accepted by them.

Would this type of relationship work for a married couple? It can and does work. Even though you are different genders, you can have a deep and secure friendship with your spouse. They can be the first person you go to when you have a problem and know that they will listen to you. They understand your heart and do what they can to protect it.

Building on the friendship

How can you be a friend to your spouse? Basically, it is the same way you are a friend to others. Be intentional on building the relationship through spending time together. Your life can become busy but showing your love and interest in your spouse by putting your time with your spouse as a priority is important. They will appreciate your conscious decision to relate to them. That is the only way you can truly get to know someone is by spending time with them. It doesn't happen by osmosis.

When you are together, what can you do to become best friends forever? I think the secret is to have an attitude of serving them. Look for ways to encourage and support them. Be available to them when they need you most. That's one comment you hear often from a person is that their friend was there for them when they struggled. A friend doesn't judge but loves always. Are you able to love your spouse completely without judging them? They most likely have faults, but you do, too. Love covers a multitude of "faults."

Can you keep a secret? Friends keep secrets when asked to do so. If you spread news about your spouse that they don't want anyone else to know, you have betrayed their trust in you. This is very hurtful in the relationship because you have shown that you do not love your spouse enough to keep their confidence.

If you have done this, it will take time to build up trust again. Be vigilant in sharing anything about your spouse.

Friends are supportive of each other's causes. If your spouse is passionate about a cause, you can show your support by helping in some way. Not only is it fun to work together, but it creates a bond of unity for the cause. It greatly encourages your spouse to have you show that you love them enough to help.

Friends laugh together. Do you find that you and your spouse share laughter? Laughter is very healing both physically and emotion- ally. It's great for the heart and blood pressure and releases endorphins that make you feel good. Emotionally it can be a release of stress that has built up over time. In fact, if you or your spouse is stressed, don't be surprised if the bout of laughter turns into tears. That is just showing the release of stress. Laughter heals.

Enjoy your friendship

The friendship you and your spouse have is special. Enjoy it. Don't set up expectations, but just let it happen. Stay close in heart to your spouse being intentional on being the best friend you can be to them. You'll be amazed at how your love grows in leaps and bounds with your best friend forever.

May God bless your home, and keep your marriage ... in Jesus' name, Amen.

Chapter 42: Be Courteous to Your Spouse's Friends and Family

Love is the condition in which the happiness of another person is essential to your own.

- Robert Heinlein

"Great news! Mom is going to come and spend the week with us." Janet announces after talking to her mother on her phone.

Sarcastically, Bob responds without looking up from the newspaper, "Oh, what great news!"

"What? Don't you want her to come visit?"

Putting the paper down, Bob looks at Janet and says, "You have to admit that your family is somewhat eccentric. They drain me of energy when I am around them for long periods of time."

"Bob, they are my family! They are a part of who I am. My family is important to me, and I thought they were to you, too."

******

Who are your favorite friends and family? They are a large part of our lives. Subconsciously, they make us who we are. We learn from everyone and become aware of what is appropriate and what isn't by their reactions to us. Good or bad, that's how we learn many things in life. There are memories that we keep in our heart that gives a special bond between these people and ourselves. In fact, losing a friend or family member causes deep grief. Life will not be the same without them. We find a new normal in our life, but it takes time for that transition to occur.

With that said, being sensitive to the friends and family of your spouse is crucial to a happy relationship. This does not mean to not share what is on your mind regarding them, but just be able to accept them in love for the sake of your spouse. It's hurtful to know that someone you love is not loved by your spouse. Your spouse can take that as a personal assessment of themselves.

Being a good host

It is an important part of many cultures to be a good host. When someone visits your home, you treat them with the best that you have, even if it is sacrificial to you. In biblical times, guests were highly regarded, and the host would even give their life so that nothing would happen to their guest. Being a host is a high calling, but does it mean only at home?

Having the attitude of a host can be for anywhere. You are acting as host with being the temple of God, so wherever your body is that is where you are the host. You are a host to all the people you encounter … including your spouse's friends and family.

Remembering that your response is your responsibility, each encounter with the people who are important to your spouse could be good. When you make the choice that you will respond in a Christ-like manner with great respect, it does not matter what the other person does. It has no effect on the decision you have already made. There is no room for blame towards anyone for your bad behavior. No one forces you to be rude and say unkind things; this happens by your own choice.

A gift of love

Knowing that certain people are important to your spouse should make them important to you. As a gift of peace to your spouse, treat these friends and relatives with the most love and respect that you can muster. Your beloved will be so happy that you are treating them in a good way. They know you are doing it for their sake and will love you for it. You are clearly giving them a huge gift of yourself by these actions, and it will be appreciated.

Being the ambassador of Christ allows you to be kind and considerate no matter what the situation is between you and your spouse's friends and family. Your important role in the scheme of all things is to live as light. What better person to do it for than your beloved?

You never know … you may change your mind about someone who at first irritated you, but now have come to truly love and respect. Being courteous in the name of Christ changes people. You may have initially thought this was for your spouse, but in the end, you may find it was for you.

May God bless your home, and keep your marriage in Jesus' name, Amen.

Chapter 43: Valentine's Day is Important!

Excitement and fire are not qualities inherent to relationships they are what happen when two people make marriage the number one priority.

- Michele Weiner-Davis

Harry looks carefully through the jewelry store to find the perfect gift for his sweetheart, his wife. A beautiful bracelet with charms lay on a black velvet setting that seem to show its exquisiteness. The charms remind him of the gift Anna is to him. One charm reads Mom, and she is a great mother to their children as she cares for them every day. Another charm is a cross reminding him of her deep devotion to God. She inspires him to keep growing in his faith.

He didn't find the price of the bracelet, so Harry asks a clerk if she had the information.

"Yes, sir. That is a beautiful choice. It costs $232. Would you like me to take it out of the case for you for closer inspection?"

Harry is taken aback by the price for a moment, but then realizes that it is Valentine's Day and his wife deserves this love piece. "Go ahead and gift wrap it," he tells the clerk.

When he arrives home, he walks into the house to find his wife dressed up to go out for their Valentine's dinner. She made reservations at a spot they used to go to when they were younger and had more money before children.

"You look beautiful," Harry said as he gave her a hug. "However, I think you need an accessory to truly bring out your beauty." He put his hand in his pocket and brings out the gift box and hands it to her.

She opens it and begins to cry. "I don't believe it. I looked at this very same bracelet last week and loved it. I never thought I would get it."

Harry is thankful for the nudge he received for Valentine's Day.

******

Have you ever been forgotten on your birthday? That is a feeling that never goes away completely. It is hurtful and you feel devalued. This is somewhat the feeling your spouse has when they are forgotten for a celebration that involves them. It's not only Valentine's Day, although this is the big "romance" holiday, but any event in their lives such as anniversaries, engagements, graduations, Christmas, or another day that means something to them.

You may think that it is too hard to remember all these dates. You can easily remember with the help of a calendar. Calendars today have many functions that help people remember appointments and special dates. Online calendars will send you an email and a pop-up reminder from your calendar. So yes, you can remember by putting a little effort into setting up your calendar. You want to make your spouse feel special and this is one way of doing it.

These are events that have touched their heart and by remembering them, you show how special you spouse is to you. Perhaps no one in their life has ever remembered these dates before. You can imagine the impact you make on their life by treasuring the days they do. They will know they are truly loved and cared for by you.

Preparing for the celebration

Give yourself at least a month to brainstorm on how you can celebrate the event in your spouse's life. Depending on what it is, you need to discern if this is a celebration for just you two, or if others should be involved. Once that is determined, you need to think about what should be done. For example, is a party in order? If it is, would it be surprise or openly planned? Food could be appetizers, desserts, barbecue, or sit-down dinner. Whatever you choose, it needs to be planned either by planning the menu or hiring a caterer.

Decorations always add to the celebration, so consider what would be appropriate. Are balloons and signs in order or something more subtle like candles and music? Also plan on having pictures taken. If you are going to be busy at the event, appoint someone to take the pictures. Your spouse will appreciate this for they can reminisce about this celebration you have given them. It is a wonderful gift.

May God bless your home, and keep your marriage ... in Jesus' name, Amen.

Chapter 44: You're wrong. Admit it!

To keep your marriage brimming, with love in the wedding cup, whenever you're wrong, admit it; whenever you're right, shut up.

- Ogden Nash

"The map shows that we need to go to the right."

Luke shook his head. "That's not the way I remember going." Nicki is getting frustrated. She had the route all mapped out, but

Luke wants to go with what he remembers. It just didn't feel right to her. But for peace in the family, she folded the map and put it in the glove compartment. "All right, we'll do it your way."

Luke sat up on the driver's seat obviously looking proud of himself. "Not to worry. We'll be there soon."

Three hours pass and they still aren't at their destination. Luke pulls over at a service station, gets out of the car, and walks into the building. Five minutes later, he returns. After getting into the car, he looks straight ahead.

"Well?" Nicki asked.

"I was wrong, and you were right. I'm sorry. We are way off track. But I now have directions to get us there."

"I accept your apology on one condition. That you give me a chance next time when I have worked on getting the directions together."

"Will do." He starts the car. Looks at her and smiles, and they continue to their destination.

******

Do you hate being wrong? Most people do, but some have a very difficult time accepting they are wrong and the other person is right

... especially if the other person is their spouse. Think about the times you have discovered you were wrong, and your spouse was right. Did you admit it? Was an apology a part of the dialogue? If not, there is room for you to grow in this area.

Ego is what blocks you from admitting the fact that you didn't have the right information. It's what keeps you from saying, "I'm sorry." It basically keeps you from growing in the area of character. So, the best solution is to get rid of it.

If you struggle with ego, what is the source of that struggle? Is it fear? Perhaps you fear you will be looked down upon if you aren't always right. Maybe you fear that you won't be respected if you are wrong. Will you be trusted? This may be another fear. All these fears have no basis because everyone is wrong at one time or another. It's called being human. You, like everyone else, are not perfect and will make mistakes. That is why you have Jesus who is full of grace that covers your errors.

Not being right about something can be a lesson. You can glean from the experience in different areas: the facts themselves, humility, appropriate response, and trusting God. As you grow in these areas, your character develops. It's about learning who you are and what you can be. It's becoming comfortable with not being perfect.

How do you become comfortable with not being right? It begins with the Word of God to build your strong foundation on the promises of Christ. Read how God was there for all of his people, no matter if they were right or wrong. There were usually consequences of wrong choices, just like we have today, but they are there to teach you the right way. What wonderful grace God gives us!

So this grace in which you are blessed can be turned into a blessing for another, such as your spouse. In realizing you are wrong, but still very much loved by God and your spouse, you can easily tell your beloved of your error. Show them that you are strong enough inside to be able to say you are wrong and to give them accolades on being right. Be filled with grace in doing this. Your spouse will appreciate it.

What if they are wrong?

If your spouse is wrong, how are you going to respond? First, think about how you want your spouse to react to your response and then decide. It is best to be kind and filled with grace. If it's not important in the realm of all things, you do not need to mention it. Why cause trouble if there is nothing to really gain from it? Because of the great love you have for your spouse, you can "forget" about the times they are wrong, and just love them.

May God bless your home, and keep your marriage ... in Jesus' name, Amen.

Chapter 45: Be Sensitive During Sex

The most desired gift of love is not diamonds or roses or chocolate. It's focused attention.

- Rick Warren

Marissa feels empty. Her husband didn't want to make love to her, but just wanted sex. Now he is turned over and snoring after he gets his fill. She feels so alone. It didn't use to be this way. He used to be caring, and the whole act of making love was so exciting. Not anymore.

******

Has sex with your spouse been building up or coursing down? If you and/or your spouse, like many other married couples, are having a difficult time with sex or simply don't want it, it's important that you both investigate the reasons you are feeling this way. You want your marriage to be at its best in all areas and especially in intimacy.

Perhaps your sex life was exciting and spontaneous at the beginning of your marriage, but for some reason, it's became dull or painful and just not worth the trouble. There could be a variety of reasons for this to occur. A visit to your doctor would be wise to see if there are any physical problems that hold you back from experiencing physical intimacy with your spouse. If there are no physical challenges, then you must look at the emotional possibilities. This is something you could discuss as a couple or talk to a marriage counselor for advice.

Be sensitive

Whatever the struggle appears to be between you and your spouse, be sensitive to them as it is worked out. Do not demean them at all in regard to sex, even if you are joking. It can do a lot more damage to your relationship as your spouse may be extra sensitive about it. You do want to treat them the best you can during this time and continually show them you love them.

Another area of sensitivity you could consider is when you are in the act of lovemaking, and you do not consider your spouse's feelings at all. If you only care about your needs being met, that message will clearly be sent to your spouse through your actions and words. This needs to change.

Put your focus on pleasing them. If that means you need to be more aggressive or gentle, then do that. If you communicate both verbally and physically of how you desire them and how happy they make you, it will be a blessing to your spouse. Have some interaction after intercourse to show them that they are more than a sex toy to you. By doing this, you increase their self-value.

If your spouse does not feel like making love, you need to respect that and not take it personally. They may not be feeling well, have a headache, or just a bad day. The mood is not there for them, understandably. Just hold them if they will allow that, rub their back or anything else that will help them feel more comfortable. Never bully them into submission. Do not make them feel stupid or tell them to "just get over it." That could destroy your relationship.

Allow them to talk it out with you if they want to. Sometimes this can help immensely by just getting the problem aired. Verbalizing it lessens its power over an individual. Ask clarifying questions and don't judge them from what they say to you. Don't be defensive, just let them talk. If there is more understanding between the two of you, this could clear up the problem. Remember; a problem shared is half solved!

You love your spouse and want them to be as happy as possible. If they feel secure in your love, that you will accept and love them no matter what, they may be able to relax and enjoy intimacy with you on a regular basis. However, if there is stress and anxiety, that make lovemaking very difficult. Be sensitive to what they need from you.

Be *thankful for the gift*

God has given you two specific gifts in this area of topic: your spouse and sex. You are both meant to enjoy these gifts. No matter what the challenge is that you might be experiencing with your spouse, be thankful. Have an attitude of praise for your spouse and for the gift of sexual intimacy with them.

If there are no issues between the two of you in regards to sex, you still need to be sensitive to your spouse's needs. Take the role of a servant in helping your spouse enjoy the intimacy you share. Sensitivity is the key to a successful intimate sexual relationship that expresses the love you have for one another.

May God bless your home, and keep your marriage ... in Jesus' name, Amen.

Chapter 46: Praying Will Bring You Closer Together

The couple who prays together – stays together.

—Unknown

"My job is driving me crazy! I don't know if I can stand it much longer," Maddie said.

John looked up from his book. "What happened today?" "Everything! The sharks in the loan department didn't like my

proposal. My assistant had to leave early today and there is a ton of

work that needs to be done. The power went out, so I lost the report I was working on. You name it, it happened."

"Honey, try to relax. Why don't you sit here near me?" He patted the couch cushion next to him.

"You don't understand, but how can you with not working in that kind of environment. It's hopeless." She sat down next to him.

He took her hand. "Maddie, nothing is impossible for God. I would like to pray with you about it. Would that be okay?"

Her eyes became teary. "You're right. That would be the best thing to do. Thank you for offering."

******

Prayer is often the most powerful thing you can do in any situation. Did you know that? Do you believe that? Do you act on that belief? Sometimes knowledge is easy but applying the knowledge to your life is the challenge. It takes an intentional choice by you to do that. Practicing this new application every day will transform it into a natural action.

Practicing prayer will build your spiritual faith into a strong force in the name of Jesus. The closer you become to God and know His voice, the stronger you will be each day. What could be better than that?

Praying together as a couple will not only bring you closer to God, but to each other. Hearing the prayers being said from the heart of your beloved is truly a wonderful thing. You will understand more of why they feel the way they do about something. The unity experienced is like none other. It is like working together on a project, fighting an issue together, or grasping an answer. You are not alone, and you have a hand to hold to remind you of that.

Becoming stronger in your relationship with your spouse can be accomplished through prayer. The Holy Spirit understands all the words spoken and unspoken that you lift to God and will work through them. Prayer is an expression of what you believe about God. It is an intimate time. Someone once said, "Prayer is a need turned heavenwards." This intimacy between a married couple is deep, and it forms a sturdy foundation in your marriage.

What should you pray about together?

The list would probably be shorter if you asked what you shouldn't pray about together. Obviously, what you can pray with your spouse is an infinite list. The Spirit will prompt both of your hearts on what to pray. One suggestion would be to read Scripture before praying. Many times, this will get your spirit ready with thoughts on what to pray. The Spirit that works in God's Word will bring it to your heart and mind connecting with your spirit. You may be amazed at how both you and your spouse are on the same track in praying. One may be thinking about a specific need just when the other speaks it. That is the work of the Holy Spirit.

Praise is another great way to start praying. Being thankful to God for all that he has done for you will lighten the burden of your worries as you remind yourself through praise that God is in control of all things. It's like thinking, "Oh, that's right … God's got it."

Don't monopolize or manipulate the prayer time together. Simple prayers are usually the best and become a sense of sharing in the time and not one being the leader and the other the follower. Do not manipulate the prayers to go the way you want them to go. Perhaps you and your spouse disagree on something. Definitely pray about it, but don't pray in an arrogant manner such as, "Please, Lord, show my wife that my way is the best way." This is not allowing the Holy Spirit to work because the focus is on you and not on God.

End the prayer time in thanksgiving. Thank God for being there while you pray and for the wonderful spouse he has provided. After the last amen, take your spouse in your arms and give them a kiss and a hug to show them how much you appreciate praying with them.

May God bless your home, and keep your marriage … in Jesus' name, Amen.

Chapter 47: Enjoy Creation Together

Love like there's no tomorrow, and if tomorrow comes, love again.

-Max Lucado

While sitting on the beach, Nate notices Rhonda on her phone again. They have been there for an hour and hardly any words were spoken to each other. Maybe he should buy a phone so she will talk to him, he thought.

"Rhonda! Put the phone away. We are here to enjoy the beach and have a good time together."

After a quick "I'll call you back," Rhonda clicks off the phone. "I'm sorry, Nate, it's just been so busy at the office, and I feel like I need to keep up on what's going on there."

"I think you need a break from the office. That's why we are here. Look … have you noticed we have sand to run in and water to splash? We had a long hard winter and now we have beautiful sunshine. Did you see it?" Nate is frustrated and pounds the sand to give emphasis to his message.

"Yes, dear, of course I see all those things and I am enjoying it. I love being here with you. I won't talk on the phone anymore while we are here. Okay?"

"Okay." Nate leans over and gives her a kiss.

Bling!

Nate looks at her and Rhonda quickly sends the call to voicemail. "I forgot to silence the phone. There, it's all set." She sees the phone vibrating on the blanket.

******

What is the best thing you like about creation? God knew that and made it just for you to enjoy. He made the mountains and valleys all by his Word. He breathed it in to being. The beauty many times can take your breath away. It's amazing all of the details that God didn't miss. They are all there. The best part about it is that you have some- one to share it with. Your spouse was created just for you and is a reflection of the wonderful love of God for you.

As a married couple, enjoying the environment and giving praise to God for it can be done in many ways. Here are a few suggestions:

Picnic – Take your beloved on a picnic somewhere picturesque. Spread out a blanket on sand or soft grass. Together enjoy the food provided along with the provision of the beauty around you. After you eat, take a walk, which is not only healthy, but will give you a chance to get a closer inspection of what is around you. Take pictures to remember this time.

Biking – This is a fun exercise to do together while reaping the benefits of the beautiful outdoors. Map out a route where you can bike and possibly some sites you will come across. This is something you can do in your community or attach the bikes on the car and go to another destination. For added adventure, you may want to try a tan- dem bike. Then you must choose who will be in the front. Maybe you can share that responsibility.

Boat ride – You and your spouse can take a ride on a canoe, paddle boat, or cruise ship. It doesn't matter, because on any of them you will enjoy the creation around you. Perhaps you can register for a dinner cruise. These are getting more popular. They are less expensive than going on a cruise, but still have some of the specialness of dining on the water.

Hiking – Going for a walk with your spouse is enjoyable and good for your health (both physically and mentally). You could plan a simple few miles to walk, or you can go for the long haul and hike all day bringing provisions to camp for the night in the beauty of the land, but do be careful of whatever creatures might be in that area. Snuggle by the campfire and look up at the stars. You are creating a memorable moment.

These are just a few suggestions of the many ways you can enjoy creation together. Be intentional in doing it for God created it for you both to enjoy. Make time in your busy schedule to go on adventures with your spouse. It will make life a lot more enjoyable for you both.

May God bless your home, and keep your marriage ... in Jesus' name, Amen.

Chapter 48: "I love you."

Any reason is a good reason and any time is a good time to say "I Love You."

-Fawn Weaver

"Have a good day!"

Carol looks at her husband, Ted, and half-heartedly says, "Yea, you too."

"What's the matter, honey?"

She turns to look at him, and wonders if she should say anything. "Well, it's just that you don't say you love me anymore. So I sometimes wonder if you do."

Ted put his briefcase on the floor. "Honey, how can you think I don't love you? I'm sorry I don't say it enough, but I truly do love you."

"It would just be good to hear it once in a while."

He hugs and kisses her. "Carol, I love you more than anything else in this world. You are my life. Thank you for marrying me."

Carol starts to laugh. "Now that's more like it."

******

There is power in words. Politicians and salespeople know this. If the words they speak make a connection to the audience the way they desire, they have won them over. Saying words and delivering them in a good manner brings more value to the words. People remember more about how the words make them feel than the actual words. That's why all people need to be careful about the words they use.

In a caring relationship, words can build up or break down the communication. This is true for words of omission, too. If there is something that your spouse needs to hear and you aren't saying it to them, that is cheating them out of seeing a fullness of your love for them. By not stating the fact that you love them daily, one can feel taken for granted, or not loved. It's so easy to do, isn't it? Even though you love them just as much as the day you married them, it's important to tell them.

Childhood experiences

Maybe you or your spouse comes from a family that didn't express affection. You may think of that as normal and showing affection as abnormal. This is a lie planted in your mind and it's time to dig it out. Affection is a biblical way in showing love. Jesus shows his affection to his disciples ... and even washes their feet.

If you or your spouse were taught that affection was not seen or heard, you or they need to be retaught and transformed to the truth of God. Read the Scriptures that talk about how Jesus held the children and blessed them, how God says and shows his love for you, and how Christians loved one another. There is affection in the words they use and in their actions. Use these texts as a model for how you can show affection to your wife as well as say it. Of course, the Song of Solomon has a lot to teach about the subject. Read that book often ... maybe together.

Practice it daily

Since there are many ways to show affection, there shouldn't be a problem finding a way to show it daily. You may say "I love you" or hold hands while watching a movie or walking. Giving a hug is always nice, too.

Practice ways of verbally telling your spouse why you love them. Is it something in their personality, or a look in their eye that makes your heart melt? Is it a word they say to you that makes your heart flip-flop? Tell them … they want to know. If all else fails, grab the book of Solomon again and start reading aloud. That will help you get started.

The important thing is to intentionally work at it. If you let it slide, you will fall back into old habits. Don't let a day go by without showing some sort of affection to your spouse. It's important communication that you need to do.

God tells us daily in his Word that he loves us. It should give you confidence and peace to know that. It's the same with your spouse. Telling them of your love takes away any doubt of your love and gives them confidence to enjoy your relationship together. The same way you can enjoy your relationship with God.

May God bless your home, and keep your marriage … in Jesus' name, Amen.

Chapter 49: There's Healing in Hugs

I got gaps; you got gaps; we fill each other's gaps.

-Rocky Balboa (Rocky, the movie)

Shannon sits in the white rocker, slowly rocking and not looking anywhere in particular. It's been a couple of days since her baby died. *Her baby died.* She can't fully come to grips with that truth. Her arms that use to hold that tiny baby so close were now empty. The emptiness sweeps through her like a cold and heartless wind chilling her to the bone.

She sees Kevin standing in the doorway of the nursery. Shannon knows that he hates to see her suffering. He seems to be at a loss of what to say or do. Pain course through him, too, and there are some days he looks so sad.

Shannon gets up from the rocker. She put her arms around Kevin and kisses him on the cheek. Filling up her arms with love is healing to her. She knows she can go on because of the love of her husband and God. Together they will mend the broken hearts they have and be able to carry on and help others who experience this type of loss.

******

How can a hug heal? It's not really the hug itself, but all the meaning that is behind it. A hug conveys feelings of love, sadness, support, and more. Think about the emotions you feel when someone hugs you. What messages do you receive? Are the messages saying that you are accepted and loved? Other messages could be as follows: I'm glad to see you. I'll miss you. You are great!

There is power in a hug. Your spouse will feel better receiving a hug from you. Whisper in their ear that everything is going to be all right as you hug them. You can be sure of your words, because with God, it will be all right.

Specific benefits

A hug has many benefits, but here are a few for you to know:

- It feels good. Not only does it raise serotonin levels to make a person feel happier, but it also helps heal negative emotions.
- Hugs can soothe an achy body because it will help them relax.
- Communication is improved between people when hugs occur because trust is built. Relationships improve from a hug.

It's definitely a booster to your relationship with your spouse to give hugs. Incidentally, there are no limits to the number of hugs you give. You will not run out of hugs, even if you do it every other minute!

Not comforable hugging?

If you or your spouse were not raised in a family that hugged, it may feel quite uncomfortable. Like discussed in the last chapter, it's a matter of getting used to it. Practicing is fun, too. Here are some suggestions for the timing of the hug.

- Early morning – Hug when you are both standing up, but not with coffee in your hands.
- Before one of you leaves – This could be for the day,

office, trip, or any other reason.

- Seeing them elsewhere – You go out for lunch and see your spouse lunching with a friend. Give them a hug.

- Welcoming them home – It nice to come home to a hug. It brings balance to the day.

- Before going to sleep – End the day with a hug (and kiss).

- When they are weeping – Comfort them with a hug. This can be very soothing.

- When they are worried – Give them peace with a hug.

These are a few suggestions, but of course there are more times you can hug ... even for no reason at all. Surprise them with a hug!

If you're in a disagreement

During a time of disagreeing, you both may not feel like hugging and that's okay. It's important to have a little distance when tempers are flared. Talk out the problem and bring reconciliation as quickly as possible. During the time where a resolution has been achieved and you want to make up, this is a great time for hugs. Just don't hug them before they are ready. Be sensitive.

May God bless your home, and keep your marriage ... in Jesus' name, Amen.

Chapter 50: Together Set Budget and Goals

The more you invest in a marriage, the more valuable it becomes.

- Amy Grant

Marj is working on the budget for the month and feels defeated. It seems like they never have enough money to do something fun, like go on a trip on a whim. They always scrap by with the money they make to pay bills.

Rick comes into the office of their home and asks, "How's it going this month?"

The look on her face gives him his answer. "Not great, eh?"

"It's not that we are going under, it's just that we don't have any extra," she said.

"This is probably a good time for us to take some time and look at everything we need to pay, what can we change, and make goals. Thank you for all the work you have put into this. I appreciate it."

"I'm glad to do it. I just get discouraged sometimes. Talking everything out sounds like a great idea to me."

******

Money, the necessary evil … right? Well, it's what the world uses so we do, too. Managing money can be difficult especially if not enough is coming in. Most times, it's the spending of the money that creates problems. Credit has been a temptation many have fallen into. Financial problems have robbed marriages of their joy. There is a better way.

The best way would be to budget and set goals before becoming married, so there are no surprises for either one of you. If you are already married, then begin where you are. There are many great resources to learn about budgeting and becoming debt-free (i.e., Dave Ramsey). Using these resources and taking a budgeting course could be helpful to you and your spouse to start again to become debt-free. It's working together on it that will make it profound for both of you. As a team, you and your spouse will create an income and pay out plan that will work perfectly for your situation.

Talking with your spouse about the budget

Talking about money can be a very sensitive topic. First, make a commitment to each other that you will be respectful of the other's choices made regarding spending and saving. It's done and in the past.

Now is the time to make new and better inroads to a debt-free life. It is possible. You can both experience this as you work together.

Begin the budgeting process with prayer. Pray that God will be the master of your money and you both will be like the servants in the parable who are given talents by the owner. You want to be good stewards of what is given to you. You will be building a plan to manage your money so it works for you and not the other way around. Many live paycheck to paycheck and have not yet discovered the way to live by investing and diversifying. Let the money do the work for you and enjoy the harvest of what it brings.

Compliment your spouse on the good choices they have made regarding money. It is so easy to focus on the bad choices made in regards to money and be angry or frustrated. That does no good in the situation. You are both on your way to making better decisions on how to save and spend. Rejoice in that fact and add the energy to make it happen. Daily there will be choices regarding money to be made. Be supportive of each other in the making of those choices. Discuss them freely together and share the times of temptation and what resulted. If they fell into the temptation, talk about how they can stand firm the next time. If they made a good choice … celebrate!

It's all in the intent

I could tell you how to set a budget, but I think I'll leave that for the experts. What I want to encourage you with is to be intentional about doing it together. Don't let it slide … it will if you let it and you'll find you haven't made a lot of progress. Continually working towards the goal is what will make things happen to your financial structure. Do not be afraid of looking deep into your financial situation. No matter what, it is fixable. God does not want you or your spouse to carry this heavy burden. He has made a way for you to be free. Take it!

May God bless your home, and keep your marriage … in Jesus' name, Amen.

Chapter 51: Counselling Helps

Don't compare your love story to those you watch in movies. They're written by screenwriters, yours is written by God.

-Unknown

Rita imagines herself as the woman in the book she is reading. The handsome cowboy wants to be with her. She tries to deny him, but his eyes, arms and lips are too tempting.

Her husband, Paul, then plops on the bed next to her tearing her out of her daydream with her cowboy. "Night, hon." He shut off the light on his side of the bed.

Rita feels empty with the reality of her marriage, which has no desire for her anymore. She wants a man to truly love her in a passionate way. She looks at her husband. He obviously can care less, she thinks. A cowboy like in her book would take her in his arms and kiss her. Why is she stuck with Paul? She needs more passion from a man.

******

Perhaps you can empathize with the feelings Rita experienced in the illustration above. Maybe you have felt hurt in this way. When you are rejected or hurt in some way by another person's words or actions, you may build up on those feelings adding other hurts to the pile and creating a huge hurt that may not have been in the current situation. For example, Rita may have been hurt by Paul's disinterested verbal and physical messages, but add on to that past similar hurts he may have unknowingly given her, plus rejection she may have felt as a child from her parents or friends. When that rejection button is hit, all the occurrences come together.

Being aware and sensitive to past hurts in your spouse's life along with current hurts will help you help your spouse move past these experiences. But it's not easy. Christian counseling could help you both become equipped with tools to handle these internal mesages that keep you and your spouse from fully enjoying life. It is well worth investigating.

The counseling process

Finding a counselor that you are both comfortable with is im- portant. You need to meet with them a couple of times to see if it is a good match. Once you find the right counselor for you both, the process can begin. What's great about a Christian counselor is that God is invited into the activity. Prayer is a part of the healing journey and Christ is given the glory, but you need to be obedient to what God is calling you to do. If the Holy Spirit is nudging you on something you need to change, do it. That will be part of the steps needed to reach the goal of healing your marriage and making it happy again.

Most sessions will probably be talking. The counselor will ask what the symptoms are now that you are both experiencing. Then they will ask some very good well thought out questions that will help you both give information to the therapist who will be able to discern action plans for you. They can help you peel back the layers of life experiences to get to the core problem and help you take it out of control over you. It is not an easy process, but the feeling of freedom experienced at the end will be heavenly for your both. Your marriage will feel so good. It will become stronger than ever. You will both also have the tools to process in a healthy manner future issues.

Working on this together is imperative to getting a whole healing for the marriage. If only one of you is committed to the counseling process, it may help, but it will not be the same outcome that could be gotten.

Through the counseling sessions you will learn how to help each other. Your communication will become better, along with your sensitivity to your mate. You will see them in a different light as you better understand who they are. Your reactions to what they say or do to you will be different, because what caused the most pain from your past will have been processed and taken out of control. You are now in control of your responses. You and your spouse can now go forward in your marriage in a strong and beautiful manner with the Lord leading the way.

May God bless your home, and keep your marriage ... in Jesus' name, Amen.

Conclusion: Is a Happy Marriage possible?

My friends, I hope you have enjoyed your journey in learning the *Essential Keys for Marital Success*. As you apply these keys to your life, you will see and experience transformation in your wedded life. If there is commitment from both partners, success is at hand. Working together and inviting Christ into the marriage will bring victory.

You can see that divorce is not the only option when struggles appear in a marriage. There is so much help available that divorce shouldn't be on the list of options for quite a while. People often think of divorce first, and that is a mistake. That is the easy way out for someone who doesn't want to work on the marriage. Your marriage is worth saving. God brought you together for a purpose that is beyond both of you. Trusting God and leaving your hurts at the cross of Christ will enable you to live your marriage free from those burdens you held onto.

It's apparent that for any marriage to succeed, God needs to be the foundation for you both to stand on. You cannot do it on your own ... it's too hard. Have you and your spouse invited Christ into your hearts and marriage? That is where you need to start. Eternal life is the gift of God for you both. Jesus died for your sins in the past, present and future. Jesus is the only way to have real peace in this world. He is the only way to have eternal life with God. It is my prayer that you and your spouse both have this unshakeable hope. If you do not have Christ as your Savior, things will be more difficult for you.

Understanding some of the concepts of this book will be difficult for they are Spirit-led. They do not make sense to a person of the world. If you haven't already, get the guaranteed eternal life with your spouse, both basking in the love of God forever. How do you do that? I have given you a sample sinner's prayer adapted for couples so that you can do this together but remember that you individually must accept Jesus.

Dear Lord, together we come to you and pray.

We know we are sinners, and we ask for your forgiveness. We believe you died for our sins and rose from the dead. We trust and follow you as our Lord and Savior. Guide our married life and help us to do your will.

In your name, amen.

If you prayed that prayer and sincerely meant it in your heart, you are a born-again creation. Welcome to the family of God! Your marriage now has the unbreakable foundation of Jesus Christ. As long as you both lean on Him, He will be there for you and help you.

Together, you now have eternal life. The peace Jesus gives you is not like the peace of the world. It is so much better. Grab onto that peace and live a married life of bliss with your beloved, the one God created just for you.

YES, a happy marriage is possible!

May God bless your home, and keep your marriage ... in Jesus' name, Amen.

Appendix

Do you know the bad thing about divorce?

If a couple divorces, they still get to run into themselves accidentally occasionally, and most times when that happens, their heart leap with freight and their blood pressure pumps faster! They never knew they would run into each other again. They keep wishing one of them would relocate out of town or better still, just die!

Divorce is a terrible thing! It is better to break several engagements than to be divorced once. It is that serious, and I don't wish it for anyone, not even for my enemies. Divorce is ugly!

Are you contemplating divorce right now? Please rethink this. Isn't there any other way out of the present issues at hand? Have you consulted God? Has God spoken? Or have your parents spoken. ***Remember: the voice of men is not always the voice of God***. Malachi 2:16 in the Message Bible reads: "I hate divorce, says the God of Israel."

Divorce may not always be the best option. Think again, perhaps you need to give it one more try!

There are several things the two of you can do to save that marriage and make it happy again. "Did I hear you say really?" YES! There really is. Reading this book and practicing what it says is one of them.

Happy couples don't divorce you know! Finding the joy together will help you both commit to the beautiful love you have for each other and to fulfill the vows you made. Don't give up. It's worth fighting for.

About the Authors

Osaro Edosa Ogbewe is a Civil Engineer by Profession and a Chartered Project Management Professional, CPMP. He is also a graduate of the Word of Faith Bible Institute; WOFBI of Living Faith Church, a.k.a. Winners' Chapel; Benin City, Nigeria; where he and his family worship. Osaro Edosa Ogbewe is also the author of *Rivers in the Desert Places*, a collection of inspirational quotes with elaborate commentaries inspired by the Holy Spirit. He also authored the poem, *"Streams in the Desert,"* which is featured in Poetry Rivals Collection 2011, published by Forward Poetry, Peterborough, United Kingdom. Also in June 2006, he won the prize for the best *"Letter of the Month"* award in Nexus magazine, an expatriate news magazine published monthly by Expat Network Limited, Croydon, United Kingdom. In 2013, the author was selected as a finalist of Africa Health Network's contest *"Health In Your Community"* organized by the Voice of America; VOA in the United States of America. Osaro is a lover of knowledge and a very strong ideologist. His most cherished virtues in life are honesty and dedication to duty, with a firm grip on the Word and fear of God. He has studied for years the various aspects to a successful marriage; and he is determined to see marriages and relationships succeed and happy. In addition to reading and writing, Osaro takes a special interest in acting in the movies. Presently the author is based in Chicago, IL USA; where he calls home. He is happily married and blessed with three children; *Spencer, Stephanie, and Michael.*

Authors' contact:

Email: **osaroogbewee@gmail.com**

Phone: +1-773-322-3979

Kathy Bruins helps writers and authors take the next step in their journey through consultation, teaching, coaching, and praying. Kathy has a freelance business and is the founder of The Well Ministries for Christian Creatives. She is the CEO of The Well Publishers. Prayer is important to Kathy. She has led many organizations in corporate prayer. Kathy serves as President of Word Weavers, West Michigan. Her speaking topics include The Book Proposal Studio, One Sheet Studio, and other helpful writingworkshops. She speaks God's truth in various topics regarding growing in faith, leadership, prayer, and writing topics.

Contact her at kbruins77@gmail.com, seeyouatthewell.net, or writingbybruins.com.

www.ingramcontent.com/pod-product-compliance
Lightning Source LLC
Chambersburg PA
CBHW061148120626
46546CB00005B/1976